About the Marine Sanctuaries Conservation Series

The National Oceanic and Atmospheric Administration's National Ocean Service (NOS) administers the National Marine Sanctuary Program (NMSP). Its mission is to identify, designate, protect and manage the ecological, recreational, research, educational, historical, and aesthetic resources and qualities of nationally significant coastal and marine areas. The existing marine sanctuaries differ widely in their natural and historical resources and include nearshore and open ocean areas ranging in size from less than one to over 5,000 square miles. Protected habitats include rocky coasts, kelp forests, coral reefs, sea grass beds, estuarine habitats, hard and soft bottom habitats, segments of whale migration routes, and shipwrecks.

Because of considerable differences in settings, resources, and threats, each marine sanctuary has a tailored management plan. Conservation, education, research, monitoring and enforcement programs vary accordingly. The integration of these programs is fundamental to marine protected area management. The Marine Sanctuaries Conservation Series reflects and supports this integration by providing a forum for publication and discussion of the complex issues currently facing the National Marine Sanctuary Program. Topics of published reports vary substantially and may include descriptions of educational programs, discussions on resource management issues, and results of scientific research and monitoring projects. The series facilitates integration of natural sciences, socioeconomic and cultural sciences, education, and policy development to accomplish the diverse needs of NOAA's resource protection mandate.

A Scientific Forum on the Gulf of Mexico: The Islands in the Stream Concept

Kim B. Ritchie
Center for Coral Reef Research
Mote Marine Laboratory

Brian D. Keller
SE Regional Science Coordinator
Office of National Marine Sanctuaries

U.S. Department of Commerce
Carlos M. Gutierrez, Secretary

National Oceanic and Atmospheric Administration
VADM Conrad C. Lautenbacher, Jr. (USN-ret.)
Under Secretary of Commerce for Oceans and Atmosphere

National Ocean Service
John H. Dunnigan, Assistant Administrator

National Marine Sanctuary Program
Daniel J. Basta, Director

Silver Spring, Maryland
July 2008

DISCLAIMER

Report content does not necessarily reflect the views and policies of the National Marine Sanctuary Program or the National Oceanic and Atmospheric Administration, nor does the mention of trade names or commercial products constitute endorsement or recommendation for use.

REPORT AVAILABILITY

Electronic copies of this report may be downloaded from the National Marine Sanctuary Program web site at www.sanctuaries.nos.noaa.gov. Hard copies may be available from the following address:

National Oceanic and Atmospheric Administration
National Marine Sanctuary Program
SSMC4, N/ORM62
1305 East-West Highway
Silver Spring, MD 20910

COVER

Gulf of Mexico image provided by Bill Kiene (NOAA) via ORBIMAGE. This image was acquired November 7th, 2004 by NASA/Goddard Space Flight Center, SeaWiFS Project.

SUGGESTED CITATION

Ritchie, K. B. and Brian D. Keller, eds. 2008. A Scientific Forum on the Gulf of Mexico: The Islands in the Stream Concept. Marine Sanctuaries Conservation Series NMSP-08-04. U.S. Department of Commerce, National Oceanic and Atmospheric Administration, National Marine Sanctuary Program, Silver Spring, MD. 105 pp.

CONTACT

Kimberly B. Ritchie, Ph.D.
Staff Scientist and Manager
Marine Microbiology Program
Center for Coral Reef Research
Mote Marine Laboratory
1600 Ken Thompson Parkway
Sarasota, FL 34236
Phone: (941) 388-4441 x353
fax: (941) 388-4312

Table of Contents

Foreward

*"If the sea floor was writ in Braille the bumps on the
bottom of the Gulf of Mexico would spell, 'Gardens of Eden.'"*
E.D. Estevez

Near the end of the last ice age, sea level was considerably lower because so much of Earth's fresh water was locked in mile-thick glaciers. The shoreline of the Gulf of Mexico was on average about 100 miles seaward of its present location; the Yucatan and Florida peninsulas were twice their present size, and Florida's coastal landscape was as arid as Mexico's is today. At sea level's lowest stand, the surface area and volume of the Gulf were substantially smaller than today, but due to the irregular bathymetry of the shelf, the ancient shoreline was approximately as long as our modern one. Early humans would eventually explore the Gulf shore as northern glaciers melted and sea level continued to rise. They used the changing shoreline as a corridor for exploration, gathering resources, and settling. The Gulf shoreline's earliest value to humans was the role it played as a connector of people to people, and people to resources.

As sea level rose, the transitions of shorelines and shallow waters to those we now see were continuous but not uniform. Rising and falling in fits and starts, the sea drowned coastal lowlands and deepened the waters over an expanding shelf zone. During this dynamic time, some short-lived barrier islands formed only to be destroyed; other, hardier islands were simply submerged. Continental rock formations near the surface of low uplands were first exposed, and then sculpted into submarine buttes and mesas by terrific tidal currents that ripped coastal land and seascapes. Shallow seafloors welled up into sun-bathed shallows as enormous geological pressure uplifted deeply buried salt deposits. And, as the waters of the Gulf warmed, yet other unusual oases of diverse and abundant marine life arose from the seabed as coral reefs.

Today, these buttes and mesas and coral reefs make up dozens of seafloor habitat islands encircling the Gulf from the Campeche Banks to the Florida Keys. They lay an average of 70 miles from today's shoreline in depths averaging 200 to 300 feet — much like a bathtub ring left by former sea levels. Each feature is relatively small, ranging in size from one-fifth of a square mile to 460 square miles. The average size of the habitat islands is probably on the order of twenty square miles, with their combined area about one-third smaller than that of Mississippi Sound, and less than one-fifth of one percent of the Gulf of Mexico's area.

While small, these habitat islands show astonishing biological productivity, owing to the structure each provides, to summits at or above the penetration of useful sunlight, and to proximity to land and continental nutrient supplies. But two attributes are even more important for the islands' evolutionary and ecological distinction — their connection through the ages, and their stepping-stone locations in the Gulf of Mexico's major patterns of ocean circulation. For thousands of years until now, they have all endured together as refugia, feeding and breeding grounds, and epicenters of productivity. They have been connected in time.

Their locations are of paramount significance for their roles as reservoirs, springboards, corridors, and destinations of marine life, including the Caribbean plants and animals swept into the Gulf through the Yucatan Strait. In U.S. waters, the habitat islands occur as elongated constellations within the western, northern, and eastern Gulf with names such as the South Texas Banks, the Pinnacles, and Pulley Ridge. Individual rises are very close together, on average only 5 to 15 miles apart, with constellations farther apart, on the order of 100 to 150 miles.

While 150 miles seems a formidable distance, it is easy work for oceanic and coastal-dwelling turtles, sharks, fishes, and mammals. In favorable currents, even passively drifting plankton can get from one to another in just a few days. And favorable indeed is the Gulf's majestic Loop Current, with its attendant eddies and whirls and gyres that sweep across the shelf on each pulse of the tide and every press of the wind. So then, these habitat islands, these constellations of the Gulf of Mexico, are connected in ecological space.

The winds and tides and currents and mounts will all endure. Whether the Gardens of Eden will is once again in human hands.

Ernest D. Estevez
Director, Coastal Ecology
Mote Marine Laboratory

Executive Summary

Overview

The Scientific Forum on the Gulf of Mexico: The Islands in the Stream Concept took place in January 2008 in Sarasota, Florida. The purpose of the meeting was to bring together scientists and managers from around the Gulf of Mexico to discuss a range of topics on our knowledge of the Gulf of Mexico, from its geology to larger-scale connectivity to the Caribbean region, and their applications to the concept of a more integrated approach to area-based management.

The forum included six panels of invited experts who spoke on the oceanographic and biological features in the Gulf of Mexico, including connections with Mexico and the Mesoamerican barrier reef system, and the legal and regulatory structure currently in place. The charge to the group was to share information, identify gaps in our knowledge, identify additional potential areas for protection, and discuss available science about connectivity and the potential value of establishing a marine protected area network in the Gulf of Mexico.

What do we know about connectivity in the Gulf of Mexico?

The basin-wide physical oceanographic processes in the Gulf of Mexico are dominated by the Loop Current and associated rings and eddies that not only dominate the Gulf interior, but also provide connectivity pathways among remote coastal and deep sea ecosystems.

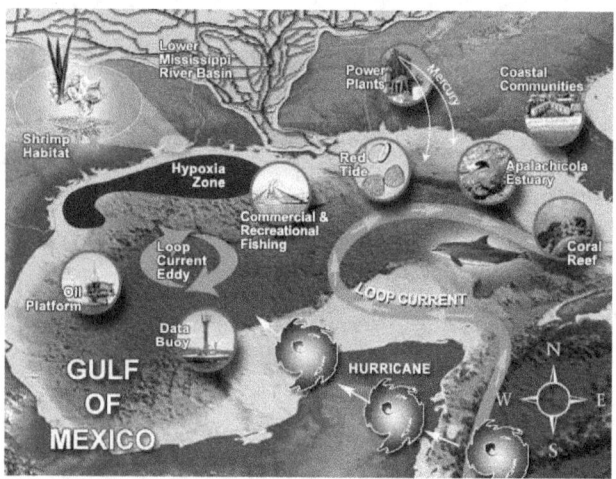

Figure by S. Murawski, provided by J. Ault

There are a number of ecologically vital, enormously productive, and scientifically interesting sites in the Gulf that are interconnected by ocean and currents and are dependent upon one another for biological recruitment and replenishment. The Gulf is also strongly linked "upstream" to the Caribbean and "downstream" to the Atlantic by the Loop Current, Florida Current and the Gulf Stream.

What do we know about unique habitats and associated marine life?

Most reefs and hard-bottom areas in the Gulf of Mexico formed on relic shorelines and barrier islands that were above sea level at some point during the past 125,000 years. Some deep reefs found in the gulf were likely formed by other physical processes such as strong currents and by gas seeping through the sediment. These areas contain a diversity of marine life. Depending on the reef, the bottom is covered by encrusting algae, sponges, soft corals and hard corals in a few shallow locations such as the Flower Garden Banks.

Recent surveys have identified many unique habitats in the gulf. For example, a survey at McGrail Bank resulted in the description of a unique *Stephanocoenia intersepta* (blushing star coral) coral reef. Pulley Ridge (eastern Gulf of Mexico) is found to the northwest of the Dry Tortugas and contains the deepest known coral reef on the continental shelf of North America. Some of these sites have already been designated as national marine sanctuaries or identified as areas of

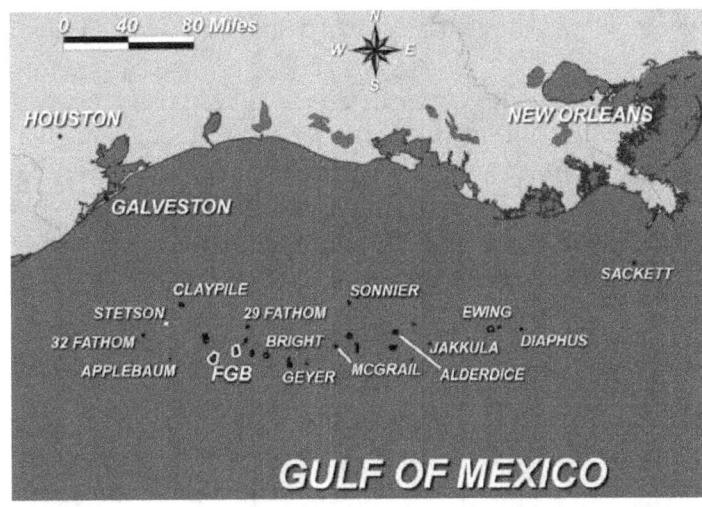

critical habitat. Most are currently afforded some degree of habitat protection by different management entities from one or more identified threats. A few areas are currently closed to fishing to protect spawning aggregations.

Gaps in our knowledge

Scientists know that there are diverse coral related resources very deep but we simply do not know if there are more "islands" out there in the stream. We should also consider the full range of biodiversity and habitats found in the region. This includes animals like seabirds and habitats such as undersea canyons. In addition, scientists need a better understanding of the complex phenomena associated with the interactions between coastal and offshore flows in the Gulf of Mexico. Having a detailed understanding of circulation patterns will help us determine how connected habitats are with one another. It will also help in understanding how adults and larvae move into, within, and out of the Gulf of Mexico.

Scientists are also still discovering new species. Cataloguing the diverse marine life found in these habitats is critical to understand how they different banks in the gulf are connected. Some locations of multi-species reef fish spawning aggregations are known but their may be other undiscovered aggregations contributing to fish populations downstream. Lastly, we need a detailed accounting

that shows where human activity is occurring throughout the Gulf of Mexico.

The potential value of a marine protected area network

We know more about the ecology and biological diversity of the Gulf of Mexico than any other comparable body of water on the planet. The scientific forum participants concluded that there was sufficient science to support the implementation of a marine protected network in the Gulf of Mexico. There are a number of ecologically vital and enormously productive sites in the Gulf that are interconnected by currents and are dependent upon one another for there well-being.

Some of these sites have already been designated as marine sanctuaries or identified as areas of critical habitat. Most are currently afforded some degree of protection by different management entities. However, we currently lack a comprehensive management approach that recognizes the interdependence of these sites across the entire Gulf of Mexico and its broader connections with the Caribbean Sea and Atlantic Ocean. By implementing an ecosystem-based management approach to the larger area of the Gulf of Mexico, a marine protected area network will be greater than the sum of its parts for two main reasons.

First, the Gulf of Mexico ecosystem is under significant human-caused and environmental stress. We must protect habitats that support the breadth of marine life found in the Gulf and also serve as refuges that can replenish other areas after significant natural or human disturbances. These places are our insurance policy to maintain the important commercial and recreational activities that depend on a healthy Gulf of Mexico ecosystem. Second, the network will enhance administrative coordination and focus additional resources to support science and management activities across the entire Gulf of Mexico. It will also facilitate increased international collaboration with our regional partners whose activities directly impacts the health of the Gulf of Mexico.

The Gulf of Mexico is a special place. It is unlike any other place on the planet and is one of the driving forces in the United States economy. It is also one of the most highly shared ocean places in the world when one considers all of the economic, recreational and scientific activities conducted within its waters. The Gulf's oil and natural gas fields support our U.S. economy. The Gulf also supports important commercial and recreational fisheries. The decline of snapper, grouper, and shark populations has had a major economic and ecological impact. The states around the Gulf of Mexico, particularly Florida, are economically dependent upon tourism, clean beaches and unpolluted waters. Now is the time to start doing things differently in marine resource protection and the Gulf of Mexico is the place where we need to start. There is an opportunity to lead the nation in terms of how we think about ocean space and how we sustain ocean ecosystems and our nation's economic vitality.

Acknowledgements

We would like to thank Sarah Fangman for compiling meeting transcripts. We thank John Armor, Donna Basso, Paula Clark, Ernie Estevez, Sarah Fangman, James Green, Rusty Holmes, Bill Kiene, Sean Morton, Joe Nickelson, Vicky Wiese, Fiona Wilmot and Trisa Wintringham for their support before, during, and after this forum. We thank Michael Murphy for drafting the executive summary. Special thanks go to Lori Arguelles with the National Marine Sanctuary Foundation, who provided material support for this scientific forum and to the many participants who contributed to discussions and scientific content of the forum outcome.

The Editors,

Kim B. Ritchie
Center for Coral Reef Research
Mote Marine Laboratory

Brian D. Keller
SE Regional Science Coordinator
Office of National Marine Sanctuaries

Organizing Committee

Kimberly B. Ritchie (Co-chair); Mote Marine Laboratory
Brian D. Keller (Co-chair); Southeast, Gulf of Mexico, and Caribbean Region;
    Office of National Marine Sanctuaries
Frank Alcock; Director, Mote Marine Policy Institute
Kumar Mahadevan, President and CEO, Mote Marine Laboratory and Aquarium
Billy D. Causey; Southeast, Gulf of Mexico, and Caribbean Region;
    Office of National Marine Sanctuaries

Welcome and Introduction

Kumar Mahadevan
President, Mote Marine Laboratory

We are honored to host this forum and to provide this opportunity to such a distinguished group of scientists and stakeholders to discuss the concept for the *Islands in the Stream* initiative in the Gulf of Mexico. There are a number of ecologically vital, enormously productive, and scientifically interesting sites in the Gulf that are interconnected by ocean and currents and are dependent upon one another for biological recruitment and replenishment. Some of these sites have already been designated as marine sanctuaries or identified as areas of critical habitat; most are currently afforded some degree of protection by different management entities from one or more identified threats. However, we currently lack a comprehensive management plan that recognizes the importance of a broader portfolio of sites in the Gulf as well as their interdependence.

The *Islands in the Stream* concept paper proposes the establishment of a robust network of marine protected areas throughout the Gulf of Mexico that will raise awareness of our "jewels of the Gulf", stimulate research, education and outreach, allow for a more comprehensive management process and strengthen some of the baseline protections that should exist throughout the network. This is an excellent opportunity to bring science into the marine policy arena and we are pleased to have our Marine Policy Institute hosting this event. I would like to recognize Dr. Frank Alcock and others in the policy program.

Mote Marine Laboratory is one of the prominent independent marine research organizations in the Gulf of Mexico region. We are dedicated to advancing marine and environmental sciences through scientific research, education and public outreach, leading to new discoveries, revitalization, and sustainability of our oceans, and greater public understanding of our marine resources. Here at Mote Marine Laboratory, the trustees, staff, volunteers and I believe that the time is ripe for a bold initiative to better protect the Gulf of Mexico's critical marine habitats and improve the management of human activities that affect them. We encourage scientific debate and discussion on the *Islands in the Stream* concept and stand ready to help implement a constructive initiative. Please accept my heartfelt thanks for your participation in this very important forum for our region and the nation.

Daniel J. Basta
Director, Office of National Marine Sanctuaries

We know a lot about the Gulf of Mexico (GOM). The GOM is one of the most well-studied and documented marine ecosystems in the U.S. For example, the GOM Atlas Project resulted in our mapping wetlands, assessing shellfish growing areas, locating the oil and gas infrastructure, and other important achievements. It is, therefore, not by happenstance that we chose it as a place to consider a network of marine protected areas.

The GOM is a special place – it is unlike any other place on the planet. It has been a driver in the evolution of the U.S. in the 20th century. If you look closely at the economic activity in the Gulf you see it is one of the driving forces in the US economy. It is also one of the most highly shared ocean places in the world when one considers all of the activities conducted in the GOM.

Now is the time to start doing things differently in marine resource protection – and the GOM is the place where we need to start. There is an opportunity to lead the Nation in terms of how we think about ocean space and how we sustain ocean ecosystems. The GOM is the place where this leadership will benefit the country the most.

Science has to connect the dots. If this idea does not have scientific voracity, it won't pass muster. It is, therefore, about the facts. We also need to determine how much information we need. What level of certainty is the scientific community willing to accept regarding connectivity? How much information do we need to "prove" that these areas are connected? Are there other areas? Are these even the right areas?

Please note, there is no official position in the Administration on this. If the Administration decides to move forward with this idea, there will be more opportunities for stakeholder involvement.

Introduction to the Forum

The Scientific Forum on the Gulf of Mexico: The Islands in the Stream Concept took place in January 2008 in Sarasota, Florida. The purpose of the meeting was to bring together a range of topics on our knowledge of the Gulf of Mexico, from its geology to larger-scale connectivity to the Caribbean region, and their applications to the concept of a more integrated approach to area-based management: the "Islands in the Stream" concept. Parts of this proceedings volume were summarized from notes taken during the forum; these sections are self-evident. The rest of the sections are manuscripts submitted by the presenters; three presenters were unable to submit contributions, but we thank them for their presentations.

The National Oceanic and Atmospheric Administration's (NOAA's) Office of National Marine Sanctuaries is developing a proposal, in conjunction with a number of partners, which is considering the concept of establishing an international network of Marine Protected Areas (MPA) around the Gulf of Mexico (Figure 1). The Gulf is one of the most scientifically investigated bodies of water in the world, yet there is still much to learn and gaps to fill regarding our scientific knowledge of the area.

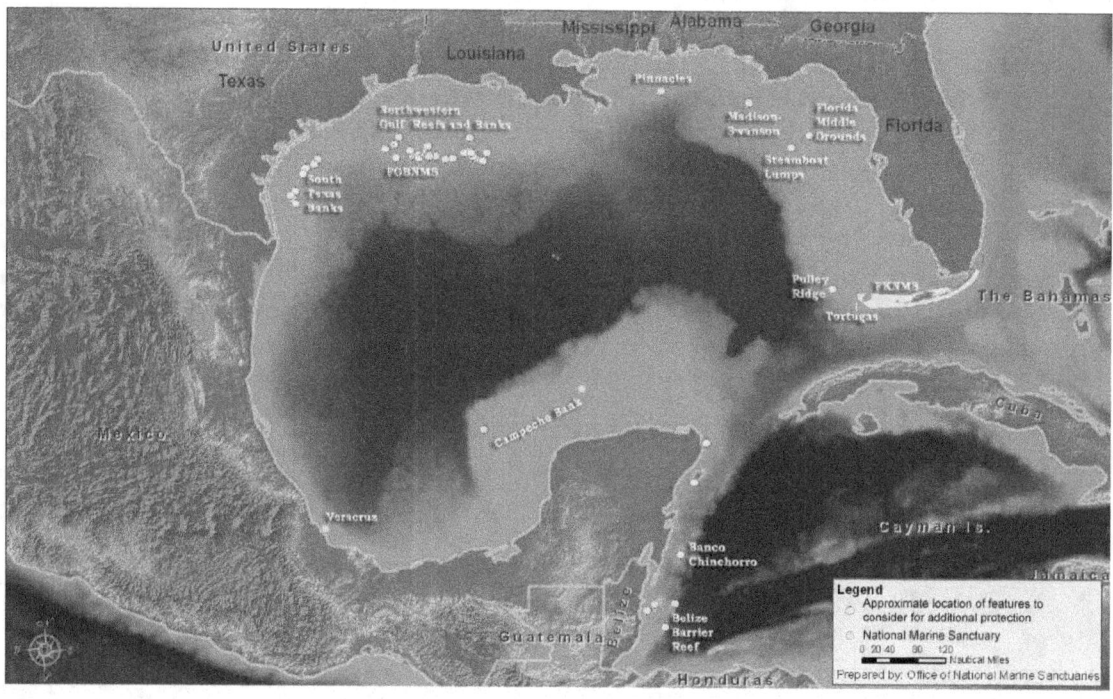

Figure 1. A map of the Gulf of Mexico, showing the proposed sites for Marine Protected Areas being assessed and considered in the Islands in the Stream: Gulf of Mexico Initiative.

Previous successful processes to establish MPAs have been those that are guided by the very best science available. This does not to imply that all of the scientific questions must be answered first, but it does recognize that science should be a major tool in citing and establishing MPAs.

Originally, the forum organizers planned to keep the invitee list to roughly three dozen scientists, but the enthusiastic interest in the topic made it necessary to include more participants. It is estimated that over 100 scientists and managers from around the Gulf of Mexico attended the science forum. The charge to the group was to share information, identify gaps in our knowledge, identify additional potential areas for protection, and discuss available science about connectivity and the potential value of the *Islands in the Stream* concept. Outcomes of the forum are this summary report, which includes research priorities that were identified, opportunities for collaborations and improvement to the concept documents.

The forum included six panels of invited experts who spoke on the geological and oceanographic features, benthic, fish and fisheries characteristics and spawning aggregations, the existing legal structure and regulations currently in place in the Gulf of Mexico, and connections with Mexico and the Mesoamerican barrier reef system. Following the panel presentations, Frank Alcock, Director of the Marine Policy Institute for Mote Marine Laboratory, facilitated an open discussion by all the attendees on information gaps, research opportunities, opportunities for collaborations, internal and external management processes, and how what is known about the Gulf supports or does not support establishment of an MPA network. This discussion was recorded and has been incorporated into this summary report.

Billy D. Causey
SE Regional Director
Office of National Marine Sanctuaries

Summary of the Scientific Forum

John Ogden
Director, Florida Institute of Oceanography

The concept of the Marine Protected Area (MPA) emerged in the latter half of the 20th century from the perception, backed by decades of scientific studies, that the marine environment was under threat and increasingly in decline from human disturbances. A MPA as defined by Presidential Executive Order 13158 is *"any area of the marine environment that has been reserved by Federal, State, territorial, tribal, or local laws or regulations to provide lasting protection for part or all of the natural and cultural resources therein."* Thus, the MPA is one type of marine managed area-- a broader category including everything from seasonal fisheries area closures to legislated marine reserves from which all take is prohibited. MPAs, belying their name, include protection but are more about governance of significant marine areas. Unlike the current fragmented, overlapping, and redundant management of marine areas by sectoral interests, such as fishing, minerals interests and recreation, the MPA broadens governance to encompass the regional marine environment, the multiplicity of human uses, and the ecosystem services which it provides to human society. The current accepted and most effective model for MPAs in the U.S. is the NOAA National Marine Sanctuary Program.

National Marine Sanctuaries are normally established by bottom up (stakeholder-driven) and occasionally by top down (legislation) policy processes. Islands in the Stream (IIS) is a special case, similar to the Papahānaumokuākea Marine National Monument which was established through the unique power of the Office of the President. The IIS proposal links nine marine managed areas, all previously established and vetted by sectoral interests, into a network. By encompassing the larger area of the Gulf of Mexico, the network will be greater than the sum of its parts for two main reasons. First, it is interconnected by physical, chemical and biological processes, building potential resistance and resilience to regional ecosystem responses to future disturbances. Second, the network will have administrative and regulatory uniformity, minimizing sectoral conflicts and administrative duplication and overlap.

The Scientific Forum was charged to analyze and discuss the biophysical background of the Gulf of Mexico with special attention to whether or not IIS was representative of the physical and biological diversity of the shallow coastal shelf. It is particularly important to understand if our knowledge of ocean currents provides sufficient evidence of the potential connectivity of the nine units of the network.

Arguably, we know more about the ecology and biological diversity of the Gulf than any other comparable body of water on the planet. The Forum emphatically concluded that there was sufficient science to support the implementation of IIS as a network of MPAs. Thanks largely to the enormous presence of the oil industry and the many universities and research institutions ringing the Gulf, there is a rich scientific background on the geological history and underlying structure, general ecological setting, and the biological diversity of the region. Much of this information can be made available in detailed, multi-layered maps of the region, providing dramatic visualization of the biophysical characteristics of the Gulf and the developing human disturbances. The sites of the Islands in the Stream rise above the sediment-dominated coastal shelf and, like islands everywhere, are refuges for biological diversity which can replenish other areas after significant natural or human disturbances. In addition to its biologically rich regional setting, the Gulf exerts a more global influence as it is strongly linked to the Atlantic by the Loop Current, the Florida Current and the Gulf Stream and is seasonally used by wide-ranging, migratory fishes and turtles as a spawning and nesting area.

The Gulf has the largest oil and natural gas fields in the world supported by huge refining and transport capacity along the coast and in major ports. The West Florida Shelf and the relatively wide shallow rim of the Gulf support important commercial and recreational fisheries and the decline of snapper, grouper, and shark populations has had a major economic and ecological impact. Florida, particularly among the Gulf states, is economically dependent upon tourism, clean beaches, and unpolluted waters. The Mississippi River, draining almost 50% of the U.S. land area, delivers sediments and pollutants originating in the grain belt to the Gulf. The "Dead Zone" an annual development of hypoxia from senescing phytoplankton blooms off the mouth of the Mississippi has increased in size and influence. The Loop Current carries these pollutants to the coral reefs of the Florida Keys and hence to the north along the east coast.

The large human presence in the Gulf suggests that the social sciences must play a strong role in the implementation of IIS. We humans are political animals who don't like surprises, tend to distrust government, and we treasure our constitutional right to make our points of view heard. Economics is the underlying driver of our society and marine governance, conservation, and sustainability must be shown to serve our needs for economic opportunity and growth. The Gulf of Mexico Alliance established by the governors of the 5 Gulf states in 2004 following the report of the Commission on Ocean Policy recognizes the importance of the Gulf and has been working effectively since then to integrate political and management efforts and focus them on the major environmental problems of the Gulf.

The IIS proposal coincides with the publication of the *Framework for Developing the National System of Marine Protected Areas*[1] by the NOAA MPA Center. The Framework, developed over 4 years by the MPA Center in consultation with the MPA Federal Advisory Committee (MPA FAC) is a guide to the scientific and social requirements for linking MPAs into a network. It outlines in detail the collaborative processes required for MPA network development across all levels of government with public participation to achieve common conservation and management objectives. It specifies the importance of clearly stated goals and objectives for MPAs and the requirements for planning, monitoring, science and adaptive management to assure stewardship and effectiveness. The IIS provides an unprecedented opportunity for the approaches developed under the MPA Executive Order to be applied to the first regional MPA network in the U.S.

The Scientific Forum concluded that implementation of IIS is urgent, given the tiny ocean area that is presently managed for conservation and sustainability and has the potential to pioneer the scientific, social and political inputs required for the implementation of MPA networks. Future large geographic scale, integrated scientific studies will bring new understanding of the ecological functioning of large marine regions. For example, as ambitious and innovative as it is, IIS is too small to encompass the life cycles of many key Gulf species which spend their juvenile lives in inshore habitats such as seagrasses and mangroves. The regional approach described in the National System Framework supports such a broader approach, outlining a process that integrates the authorities and capabilities of state and federal agencies, along with those of the private and academic sectors to help undertake a truly ecosystem approach to management. It is clear that new approaches and techniques will be needed to address future problems in management and mitigation of human impacts to the oceans.

I am reminded of the creation of the National Wildlife Refuges by President Teddy Roosevelt at the beginning of the last century. By enlisting hunters and fishermen as allies in this effort, he was successful in beginning a process that, including National Parks, National Forests, and Bureau of Land Management, protects and manages a total of almost 30% of the land area of the U.S. We stand at a point in time where our oceans, approximately 120% of the U.S. land area[2], demand similar attention to management and protection and it will require similar coalitions of interest groups to achieve success.

References

[1] Framework for Developing the National System of Marine Protected Areas (in press). National Marine Protected Areas Center, NOAA's Office of Ocean and Coastal Resource Management, Silver Spring, MD www.MPA.gov

[2] U.S. ocean area may be defined as the area of the Exclusive Economic Zone, from the shoreline to 200 nautical miles.

Panel 1: The Geological Setting

Moderator: Brian Keller

Geologic Underpinnings of the "Islands in the Stream"; West Florida Margin

Albert C. Hine and Stanley D. Locker

College of Marine Science, University of South Florida, St. Petersburg, FL

Hard Substrate--The "Islands of the Stream" concept is entirely appropriate in that much of the substrate supporting relict and modern coral reefs are drowned shorelines and barrier islands. Multiple paleo-shorelines on the west Florida shelf formed as a result of: (1) carbonate sediment production in the nearshore environment, (2) stable sea-level (stillstand), and (3) rapid cementation. During sea-level stillstands, carbonate skeletal sediments produced by the nearshore benthic community were transported by shoaling waves to build beaches and subaerial dunes. Carbonate sediments, particularly those made of aragonite and high Mg calcite, are chemically reactive subject to dissolution and precipitation both in the marine and fresh groundwater environments. As a result, relatively newly-deposited carbonate sediments became cemented by interstitial carbonate crystals forming erosionally-resistant limestone.

When sea-level began to rise after a stillstand, the migrating surf-zone did not erode the shorelines, but inundated them thus leaving a marine hardbottom available for colonization of benthic organisms. In the southern Pulley Ridge area, in particular, the deep (60-70 m) living reef community is clearly situated on a 30 km long, 5 km wide, and 2-3 m high beach ridge-dominated barrier island. Since the barrier-island morphology is so clearly imaged, we conclude that this deep reef is very thin (~.5 m) and forms a geologic horizontally-distributed biostrome rather than a vertically-erect bioherm.

The linear reef-like features at Madison Swanson and maybe Steamboat Lumps also occupy paleo-shorelines. Madison-Swanson, in particular, is situated on a sea-level lowstand river deltas the top of which probably began to produce carbonate sediments when sea-level started to rise thus shutting down fluvial influence. However, the geologic underpinnings of other reefs such as the Florida Middle Ground, Howell Hook, or the outlier reefs are not well known since the appropriate rock cores have not be obtained.

The newly discovered Sticky Grounds (Figure 1) form a narrow band (2 km) of "seismic" patch reefs (~5 m relief) that must have initiated growth on a nearshore hard substrate. High-resolution seismic reflection data clearly show water-column acoustic anomalies that may be gas bubbles escaping from many of the individual rocky structures. They do not appear to be fish. If so, we speculate that methane seeps might have played a role in carbonate cementation and hard substrate generation. A "seismic" reef is a feature seen in acoustic remote sensing that very closely resembles reefs seen in other remote sensing data that have proven to be reefs through ground-truthing and direct sampling. If this hypothesis is proven, it would be the first example of a reef system on the west Florida margin that owes its origin to gas seeps.

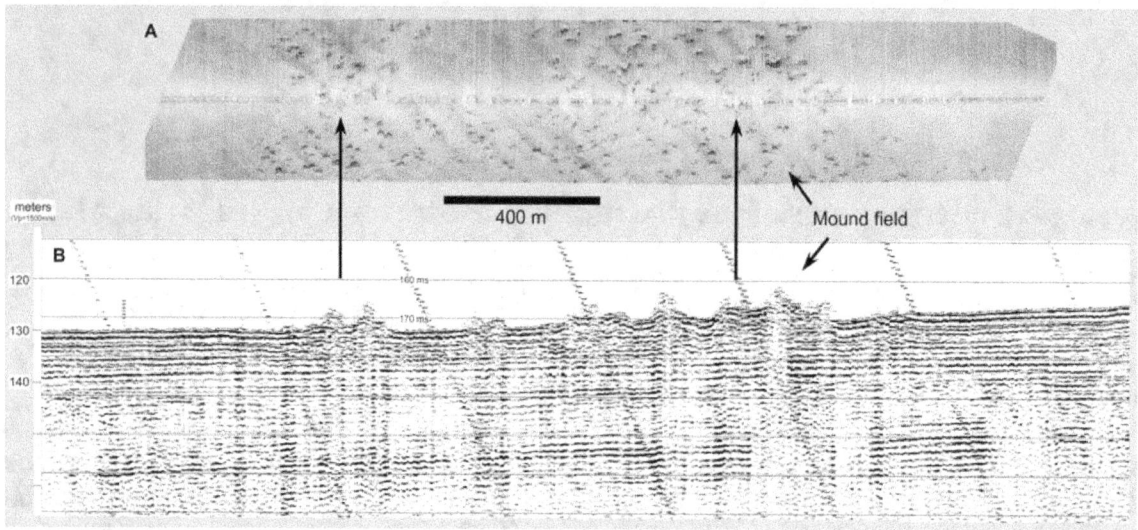

Figure 1. Side-scan sonar and high resolution seismic images of the seismic patch reefs at the Sticky Grounds. These features are a new discovery. We do not know what benthic or fish communities are supported, although dredge hauls indicate that no living corals exist. But, the mounds are indeed rocky. Water column anomalies seen in seismic data suggest that gas seeps might be present.

Sea Level--The distribution of hardbottoms and reefs is dependent upon sea-level history—at least for the past 125 thousand years ago and perhaps even further back in time. The islands forming the upper Florida Keys are coral reefs that grew during the last interglacial event when sea level was ~6 m higher than today. The outlier reefs that lie seaward of the main Keys reef tract and extend west beyond the Dry Tortugas formed ~85 thousand years ago when sea-level was ~10 m lower than today. Possibly, the Florida Middle Ground complex formed at this time, but absence of rock coring and appropriate age-dating precludes a definite age determination.

During the Last Glacial Maximum (LGM; marine isotope stage 2) at ~18ka when sea level was ~125 m lower than today, the Sticky Grounds probably formed in the nearshore. We have named this zone of many dozens of seismic patch reefs the "Sticky Grounds" since fisherman frequently have had their gear stick to the bottom due to the obvious roughness (Figure 1).

We speculate that seismic reefs formed southern Howell Hook during the LGM as well, but we have no samples to date (Figure 2). These seismic reefs are enigmatic in that they extend down to -165 m. If they, indeed, formed during the LGM, they must have formed in at least 35 m of water suggesting extreme water clarity at that time. These features and the surrounding margin appear to have been severely eroded by the Loop Current impinging upon the upper slope.

At the end of the LGM rapid melting of continental ice sheets forced global sea level to rise rapidly after ~18 ky. During this deglaciation, there were short periods of sea-level stillstand followed by rapid melt-water pulses causing sudden rises in sea-level—all indicating the non-linear manner in which the ice sheets disintegrated. It was during these multiple stillstands that shorelines and barrier islands were formed on the west Florida shelf. Age dating of a series of shorelines seaward of Key West reveals three periods of fluctuations between 14 and 13 thousand years ago. It was during this time we suggest (jump correlation) that the Pulley Ridge barrier island formed. Pulley Ridge is at the same depth as these features off Key West, but we do not have the appropriate samples to date. So, we make the tentative assumption that they are same age.

By ~9 ka many of the other reefs in south Florida outside of the Islands in the Stream area such as the small reef banks at Riley's Hump, Tortugas Bank, Dry Tortugas, and the Florida Keys reef tract started to form.

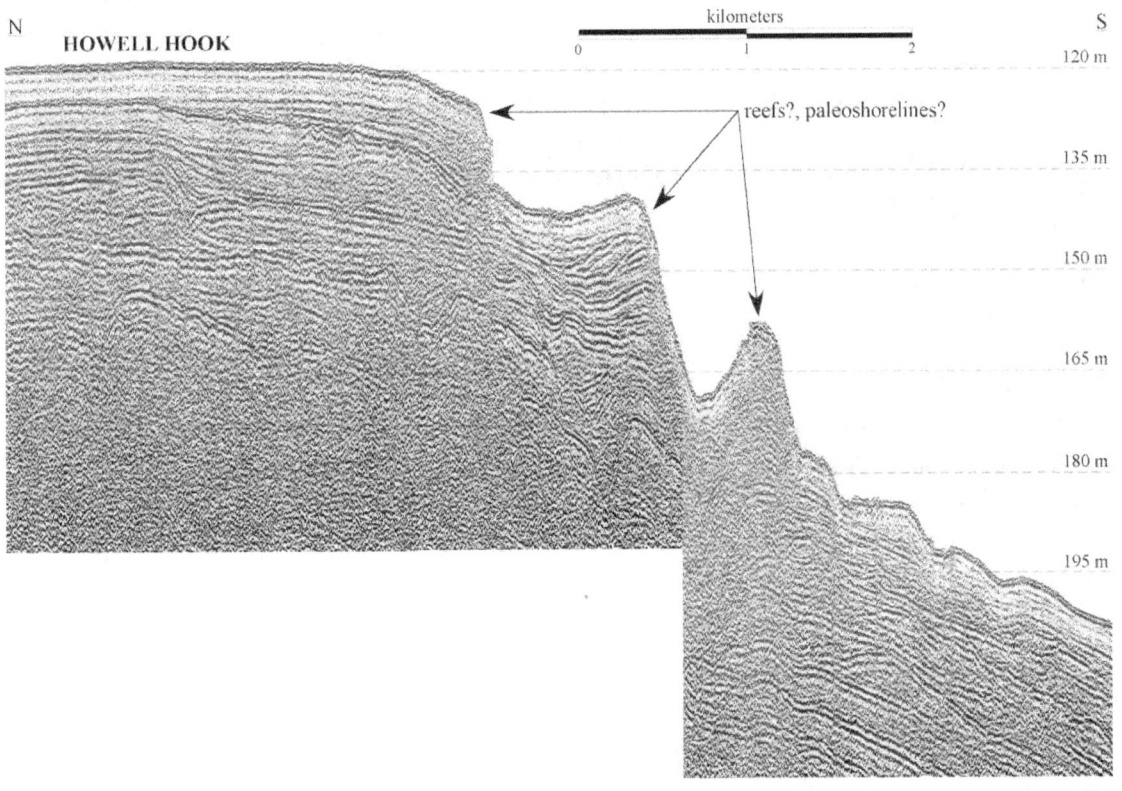

Figure 2. High-resolution image of seismic reefs at Howell Hook. This is also a new discovery. We know very little of these features and if they support some benthic and fish community. It appears that erosion, perhaps by the Loop Current, has been pervasive in the past.

Oceanography--In addition to hard substrates formed by carbonate sedimentation/cementation spatially and temporally distributed by sea-level history, favorable water column conditions for coral reef growth are required.

The 30 m deep Florida Middle Ground reef structures must have been formed when favorable water conditions bathed this area since no reef framework is being constructed presently. Perhaps, these reefs formed during marine isotope stage 5a (~80 thousand years ago) when sea-level was somewhat lower than today's highstand. These features seem too well developed and too extensive to have formed during the very late Pleistocene/very early Holocene (~10 thousand years ago).

During the LGM (~18 thousand years ago) sea level stood ~125 m lower than today and oceanographic conditions were favorable for reef development at the Sticky Grounds and southern Howell Hook. If confirmed by rock sampling and drilling, this would be a new discovery suggesting that reefs could grow in the eastern Gulf of Mexico during at this time.

The deep, light-dependent coral reef at southern Pulley Ridge exists because of being bathed by persistently clear and warm water over century if not millennial time scales. At some point in time after inundation of the cemented barrier island some 13 thousand years ago, the Loop Current began to intrude up onto the margin as a result of deepening water due to sea-level rise. When this occurred, we speculate that more turbid and more nutrient rich shelf waters were replaced by clearer, oligotrophic waters of this component of the western boundary current. For sure, modern oceanographic measurements illustrating the 3D structure of the water column are essential. The hardgrounds at Madison Swanson and Steamboat Lumps may have formed in this time frame as well (14-13 thousand years ago).

What's next?--We will not be able to understand the earth better until we can image it better. The space program, using the Hubble Telescope and the satellite probes to planets and their moons in our Solar System, clearly demonstrates this point. We propose more extensive seafloor mapping using side-scan, swath bathymetry, high-resolution seismic reflection profiling, bottom-classification geoacoustics and appropriate bottom camera/TV imagery and direct sea-floor sampling in strategically selected areas. We simply do not know if there are more "islands" out there in the stream.

References

Hine, A.C., and Locker, S.D., in press, The Florida Gulf of Mexico continental shelf—great contrasts and significant transitions, in, Holmes, C.E., ed., *Gulf of Mexico—Geology: Fisheries Volume Bulletin* 89, Harte Institute, Texas A&M University Press.

Hine, A.C., Halley, R.B., Locker, S.D., Jarett, B. D., Jaap, W.C., Mallinson, D. J., Ciembronowicz, K.T., Ogden, N.B., Donahue, B.T., and Naar, D.F., in press, Coral reefs, present and past, on the West Florida Shelf and platform margin, in Riegel, B., and Dodge, R. (eds.), *Proceedings of the 11ᵗʰ Coral Reef Symposium*. Springer Verlag.

Jarrett, B.D., Hine, A.C., Halley, R.B., Naar, D.F., Locker, S.D., Neumann, A.C., Twichell, D., Hu, C., Donahue, B.T., Palandro, D., and Jaap, W.C., 2005, Strange bedfellows—a deep hermatypic coral reef superimposed on a drowned barrier island; southern Pulley Ridge, SW Florida platform margin: *Marine Geology*. v. 214, p. 295-307.

Lidz, B. H., Shinn, E.A., Hine, A.C., and Locker, S.D., 1997, Contrasts within an outlier-reef system: evidence for differential Quaternary evolution, south Florida: *Journal of Coastal Research*. v. 13, p. 711-731.

Locker, S.D., Hine, A.C., Tedesco, L.P., and Shinn, E.A., 1996, Magnitude and timing of episodic sea-level rise during the last deglaciation: *Geology*. v. 24, p. 827-830.

Mallinson, D. Hine, A.C., Hallock, P., Locker, S.D., Shinn, E.A., Naar, D.F., Donahue, B., and Weaver, D., 2003, Development of small carbonate banks on the south Florida platform margin: response to sea level and climate change: *Marine Geology*. v. 199, p. 45-63.

Habitat Islands along the Shelf Edge of the Northwestern Gulf of Mexico

Niall C. Slowey[1], Troy Holcombe[1], Mark P. Betts[2], and William R. Bryant[1]
[1]Department of Oceanography, Texas A&M University, College Station, TX
[2]Devon Energy Corporation, Houston TX

Numerous reefs and banks occur along the edge of the continental shelf of the northwestern Gulf of Mexico. Investigations have shown that these seafloor features contain significant marine resources. Several banks, including the East and West Flower Gardens, possess some of the healthiest coral reef communities in the United States. All of these features provide crucial habitat for a variety of fish and invertebrate species of commercial and recreational importance. Recently collected data suggests that the marine habitats situated at these reefs and banks are not completely isolated from each other; rather, a network of seafloor ridges and outcrops, which act as physical links and provide additional valuable habitat, connects these important marine areas. To understand how these "islands" of habitat originated and how they are influenced by environmental processes today, it is necessary to consider the geologic setting of the seaward edge of the continental shelf and the upper continental slope.

The continental shelf of the northwestern Gulf of Mexico (named the Texas-Louisiana Shelf) extends nearly 1000 km from the delta of the Mississippi River westward to the Rio Grande River. It is quite broad and gently sloping; its width ranges from about 100 km at its eastern and western ends to nearly 200 km at its center, and the boundary between the seaward edge of the shelf and the upper edge of the continental slope occurs between 120 and 200 m water depth. A number of banks occur on the seafloor along the length of the shelf edge (Figure 1). Depending

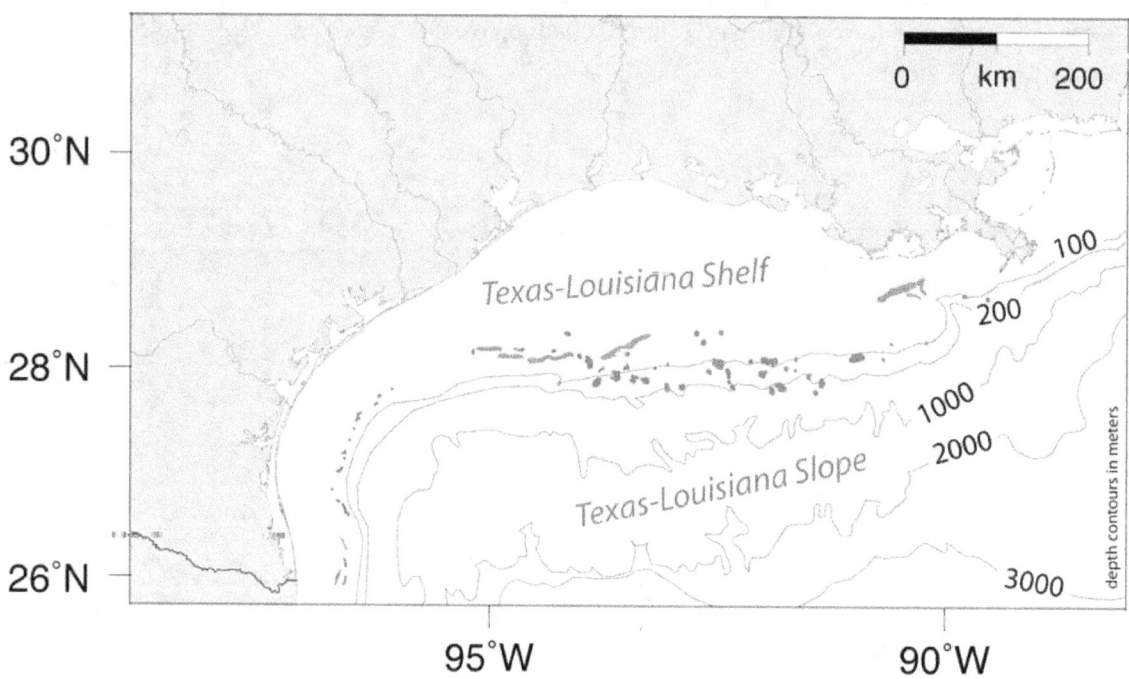

Figure 1. Locations of the larger "banks" occurring along the seaward edge of the Texas-Louisiana Shelf in the northwestern Gulf of Mexico. They are comprised of two types of physiographic features, banks (red) and ridges (blue), which are identified based upon patterns of seafloor bathymetric relief.

on what criteria are used to classify these features, various compilations have counted from 65 to over 200 shelf edge banks. Their dimensions are quite variable; their maximum vertical relief may range from a few to over 100 m and their area may be as great as many 10's of km^2. These physiographic features and the corresponding occurrence of coral reefs and other habitat types reflect several primary geological influences.

Sometime between the last glaciation and today (i.e., the past 20 kyr), seafloor environmental conditions at these banks allowed biological communities to become established and sustain steady growth. A number of environmental conditions must exist for this to happen, including the following: (1) The seafloor must offer the organisms a firm substrate for attachment. (2) Seawater circulation must be vigorous so the physical parameters of the environment meet the needs of the organisms. (3) The turbidity of the seawater must be sufficiently low. These conditions can occur when the seafloor exhibits bathymetric relief and sites are raised above the surrounding seafloor. The geologic processes that create seafloor physiographic features with bathymetric relief often expose stiff, partially-lithified sediments or rocks at seafloor, providing firm substrate for benthic organisms. Raised sites are exposed to the stronger circulation that occurs in the water column and may avoid the higher levels of turbidity that occur at relatively flat areas of the seafloor due to the influx of terrigenous sediments via rivers and the interaction of waves and the seafloor.

Many of the banks and other seafloor features that exhibit bathymeric relief exist as a consequence of the movement of allochthonous salt within the seabed (Figure 2). It is generally thought that as the Gulf of Mexico basin opened during the Late Triassic and Early to Middle Jurassic periods (over 160 million years ago), the passages between the basin and the adjacent

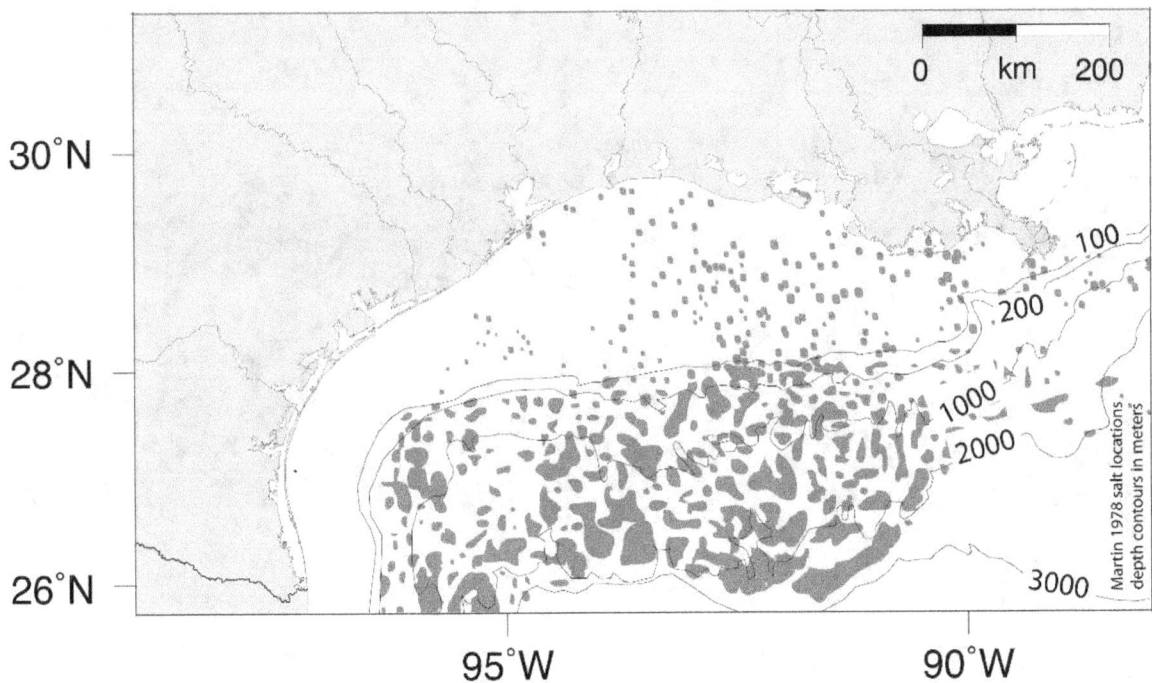

Figure 2. Locations of bodies of allochthonous salt in the seabed that occur close to the seafloor of the northwestern Gulf of Mexico.

Pacific Ocean were restricted so that the seawaters within the basin were in only intermittent communication with those outside of it. Under the prevailing warm and dry climatic conditions, evaporation of seawater led to the precipitation and accumulation of the Louann Salt and other age-equivalent salt deposits on the floor of the north region of the basin. Over time this salt was buried beneath great sequences of sediments; when exposed to high pressure and temperature upon burial, the salt has acted in a plastic fashion and flowed both upward and laterally in a seaward direction. These salt deposits are in places several km thick and span a vast area that today underlies much of the coastal plain, continental shelf, continental slope, and continental rise of the northwestern Gulf of Mexico.

Along the seaward edge of the continental shelf and the upper continental slope, discrete stocks and plugs of rising allochthonous salt have pushed overlying sediments upward, creating domes that rise above the surrounding seafloor (Figure 3). Analyses of the features of shelf-edge banks along the eastern and central portions of the Texas-Louisiana Shelf (e.g., direct observations, seafloor bathymetry, gravity anomalies, heatflow values, sub-seafloor seismic reflection data, rock samples, etc.) indicate that such salt diapirism is the process by which most of these banks originated. Several examples of salt-related bank features are presented in Figure 4.

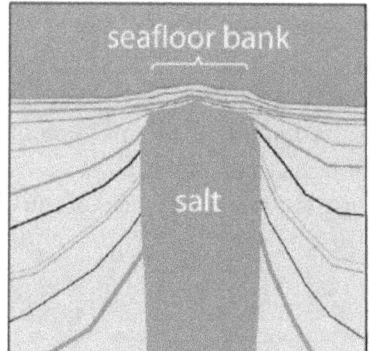

Figure 3. Schematic illustration showing how stocks and plugs of allochthonous salt rise upward from underlying massive salt deposits, pushing seabed sediments upward in a domed fashion to create the seafloor relief that defines many banks along the seaward edge of the eastern and central portions of the Texas-Louisiana Shelf.

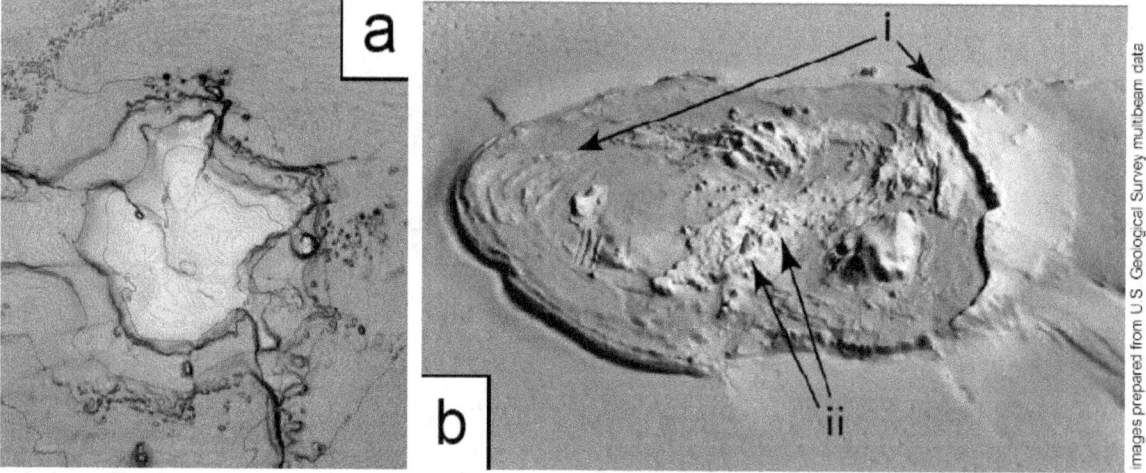

Figure 4. (a) The radial pattern of ridges evident in the seafloor bathymetry of Bright Bank is consistent with the radial faulting and uplifting/down-dropping of blocks of the seabed that are characteristics of salt diapirism. (b) The near circular outline of the Alderdice Bank and the partially-eroded, exposed layers of concentrically-domed seabed sediments [i] along with the occurrence of basalt spires [ii] indicate that Alderdice Bank formed as allochthonous salt rose and moved laterally over 100 km carrying entrained Cretaceous igneous material to the seafloor.

By creating banks, rising allochthonous salt certainly plays a crucial role in creation of valuable seafloor habitat in the northwestern Gulf of Mexico. Bright Bank, East Flower Garden Bank, West Flower Garden Bank, Stetson Bank, are among the banks that have living hermatypic corals, and many banks now support communities fish and invertebrate species.

Rising allochthonous salt can also play a secondary role in habitat formation. Salt dissolves when it comes into contact with seawater circulating along fault planes or when it is exposed to ambient seawater at the seafloor. East Flower Garden Bank illustrates two ways that salt dissolution affects seafloor habitat (Figure 5). Loss of salt from the seabed can alter the seafloor by causing overlying sediments to collapse and depressions to form in the seafloor. The presence of dense brine produced via dissolution can create a local environment where communities of organisms relying on chemoautotrophic processes thrive. If the brine pools in seafloor depressions, anoxic conditions can also become established.

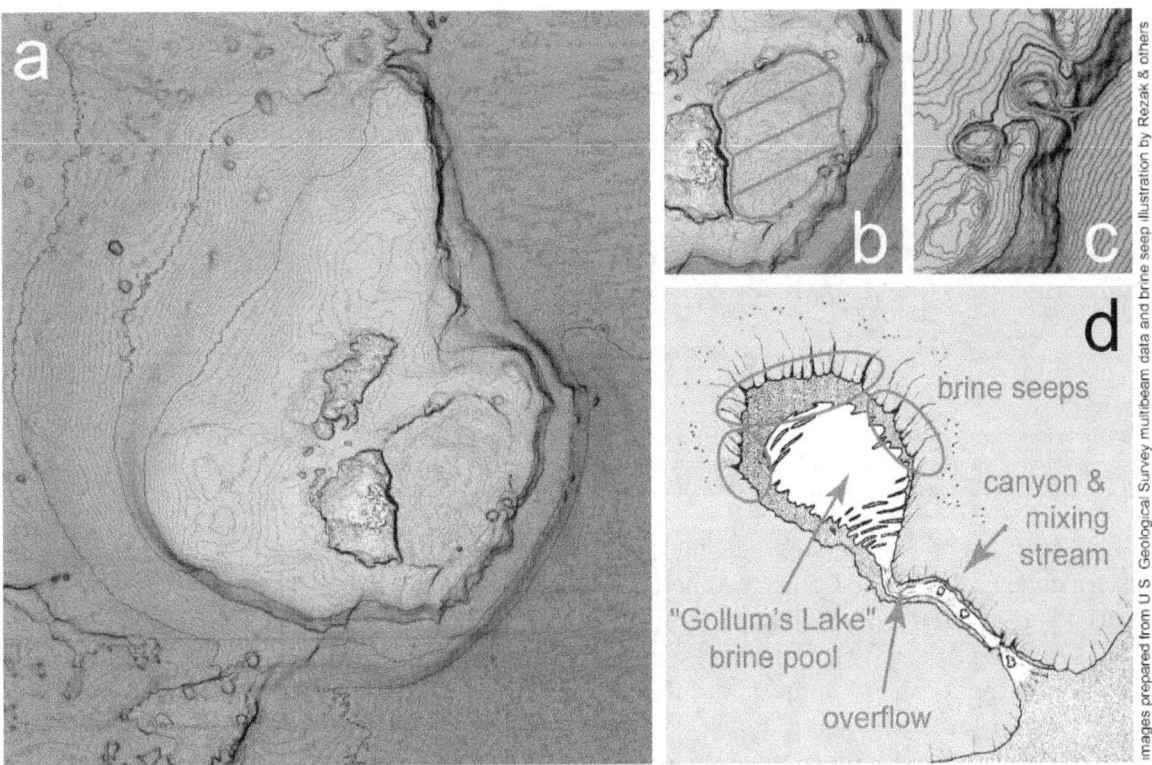

Figure 5. Seafloor features of East Flower Garden Bank reflect the dissolution of allochthonous salt: (a) Seafloor bathymetry of the bank. (b) Large depression at the southeastern portion of the bank due to dissolution of salt in the seabed. (c) Small depressions along southeastern edge of the bank where brine from the seabed exits onto the seafloor. (d) Geomorphologic features associated with brine exiting onto the seafloor and then flowing off of the bank.

Unlike the banks on the eastern and central edges of the Texas-Louisiana Shelf, shallow salt bodies do not occur beneath banks on the western edge of the shelf (compare Figures 1 and 2). Other geologic processes must therefore be responsible for the formation of these banks.

Important clues about the origins and histories of the banks are provided by samples collected from the seafloor and seismic profile images of the banks and surrounding seabed. Material dredged from the surface of several banks shows that they are covered by calcium carbonate derived from reef-dwelling organisms, including coral skeletons and coralline algae nodules. A seismic reflection profile across Baker Bank (Figure 6) shows the bathymetric relief associated with the bank at the top of the profile, which corresponds to the present-day seafloor, and the mass of carbonate comprising the bank is evident as chaotic seismic reflectors just below the seafloor. The existence of laterally continuous seismic reflectors underneath the bank indicates that seabed upon which the bank formed was not deformed significantly by shallow salt diapirism (as is the case for eastern and central portions of shelf edge). Faulting of the seabed has caused some relative vertical motion of portions of the seabed, though these effects are most apparent deep within the seabed and minimal near the seafloor. Nevertheless, subtle bathymetric relief (perhaps created by faulting, differential compaction/erosion of subaerially exposed river delta sediments during the glaciation, or erosion/mass-wasting at the seafloor) must have been sufficient for reef organisms to become established.

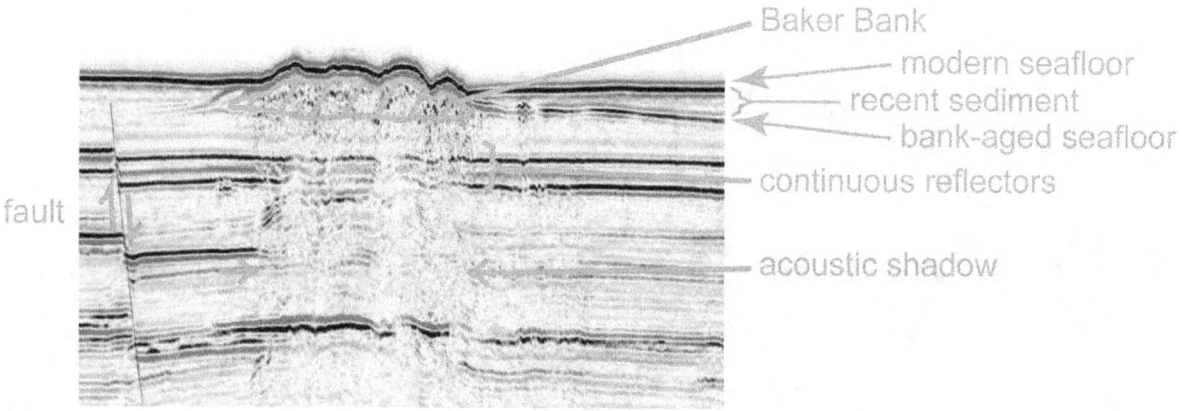

Figure 6. Seismic profile of Baker Bank, illustrating several features of the banks that occur along the seaward edge of the western portion of the Texas-Louisiana Shelf. Note that the vertical scale of the profile is exaggerated relative to the horizontal scale and acoustic shadowing can make sediment horizons that are continuous appear distorted.

Several samples of reef-derived calcium carbonate dredged from the surfaces of banks on the western edge of the Texas-Louisiana Shelf were radiometrically dated. The most recently formed material was a *Siderastrea siderea* coral from Dream Bank that yielded a calibrated age of about 12 kyrs before present. This time corresponds to the early portion of the transition from the last glaciation to today when sea level was about 60 m lower than it is today (during the last glacial maximum sea level was about 120 lower than it is today). The western-shelf edge banks are about 60 to 80 m deep now so the organisms that formed these banks lived within a few 10's of m of the sea surface. However, while communities of reef organisms once grew on these banks, they failed to survive the changes in local environmental conditions that occurred as sea level rose to its present position. Sediments deposited since the reefs stopped growing are draped onto the side of Baker Bank (Figure 6). Presumably, the either the growth of the reef organisms could not keep pace with the rise of sea level, or the turbidity of the water became too great for the reef organisms as sea level rose and flooded the continental shelf.

References

Beaudoin, J., J. Gardner and J. Hughes Clarke, 2002, Bathymetry and acoustic backscatter of selected areas of the outer continental shelf, northwestern Gulf of Mexico, *Cruise report R/V Ocean Surveyor O1-02-GM, U. S. Geological Survey open-file report OF02-410.*

Fairbanks, R., 1989, A 17000-year glaciao-eustatic sea level record: influence of glacial melting rates on the Younger Dryas event and deep-ocean circulation, *Nature* v. 342, p. 637-642.

Holcombe, T., L. Holcombe, W. Bryant, and S. Bednarz, 2006, *Northwest Gulf of Mexico Continental Slope and Shelf Edge Banks, Bathymetric Imagery from Multibeam Surveys*, College Station, TX, Texas Sea Grant College Program, CD-ROM, 5p. text, 52 images, index map, gazetteer.

Holcombe, T., L.Holcombe, W. Bryant, and S. Bednarz, 2007, *Bathymetry of the Northwestern Gulf of Mexico Continental Shelf, Including Topography of Adjacent Coastal Land Areas of Texas and Louisiana*, College Station, TX, Texas Sea Grant College Program, CD-ROM, 8p. text, 38 images, index map.

Martin, R., Jr., 1980, Distribution of salt structures in the Gulf of Mexico, *U. S. Geological Survey, Map MF-1213.*

Rezak, R., T. Bright, and D. McGrail, 1983, *Reefs and banks of the Northwestern Gulf of Mexico*, John Wiley & Sons, New York, 256 pp.

Salvador, A. (editor), 1986, *The Gulf of Mexico Basin*, The Geological Society of America, Boulder, 568 pp.

Winker, C., and J. Booth, 2000, Sedimentary dynamics of the salt-dominated continental slope, Gulf of Mexico: integration of observations from the seafloor, near-surface, and deep subsurface, *Proceedings of the GCSSEPM Foundation 20th Annual Research Conference Deep-Water Reservoirs of the World, 3-6 December 2000*, p. 1059-1086, CDROM publication.

Panel 1 Discussion

Al Hine (University of South Florida) – presentation/ panelist
Niall Slowey (Texas A&M University) – presentation/ panelist
Gene Shinn (University of South Florida) – panelist

(from meeting transcripts)

Billy Causey: The "moat" effect at Pulley Ridge – could that be causing what you saw at Hollow Hook?

Al Hine: I don't think so. I think it is erosion.

Niall Slowey: Could it be like what is happening on the Great Bahama Bank?

Al Hine: (not captured)

Gene Shinn: You said the Florida Middle Grounds are being degraded?

Al Hine: In terms of being eroded. Sediments are being generated and then being carried in a net southeast flow – that net flow can bury the lower relief features. All the multibeam evidence shows that they are shrinking. There is stuff growing on them, but they are being eroded away. They formed around 80 or 90 million years ago. The Florida Middle Grounds are enigmatic.

Tony Grogan: What period of time was the degradation and did human activity have anything to do with it?

Al Hine: No.

Question: Are the salt diapirs influencing the benthic habitat?

Niall Slowey: (not captured).

Andy Shepard: Are we missing any geologic features that we should consider adding to the network?

Al Hine: I have restricted my remarks to 160 meters or less, however there are deeper features. The *Lophilia/Dendrophilia* reefs. The "Sticky Grounds" was a surprise. We didn't predict that at all. Same with Pulley Ridge – we wanted to see where the Florida Reef Tract ended and we found Pulley Ridge. The West Florida Shelf is a huge area – bigger than the state of Florida. We need more imagery. We are in reconnaissance mode and have been for some time.

Ian MacDonald: There are very productive areas in the deeper regions of theGulf of Mexico – how deep do we want to go?

Niall Slowey: You could go to 3000 meters.

Ian MacDonald: There is no geologic reason to cut off?

Niall Slowey: There are diverse coral related resources very deep; it becomes a question of practicality.

Jim Culter: The proprietary information – will the public have to recreate the information that is already there?

Niall Slowey: Most information the oil industry has doesn't have great financial information. So it is available.

Steven Atran: (The Gulf of Mexico/Florida Middle Grounds) Last year we had a few events in the gulf referred to as earthquakes. Are these things that can be predicted or monitored?

Al Hine: The US Geological Survey explanation was that it was 3200 meters of water, sediment cover was very thick; it occurred off here, and the epicenter was right at the bottom of the sediment column and on ocean crust. There are old faults that traverse thru the crust. Here you have a huge weight on these old faults. This has happened in the past.

Niall Slowey: There are always earthquakes in the Gulf of Mexico – they just aren't big enough for you to notice. They are due to the salt movements. Very difficult to model and predict.

Steven Atran: Is there any danger that some of our reefs will collapse on us?

Gene Shinn: There was an earthquake that was felt from Key West to Tampa. These have happened before.

Dan Basta: Great interest today is climate change. Relic shorelines are useful to look at climate change. Are there relic shorelines in the Gulf of Mexico that are well defined?

Al Hine: We have shown how the sea level rose – but in a series of jerks. It created a shoreline every time and we can date them. There is a clear record of something about ice dynamics that is non- linear. It won't occur on a straight line – geology clearly shows that you can have rapid sea level rise – could go into a runaway mode for a hundred years.

Niall Slowey: The Gulf of Mexico is one of the best places you can do this. Listed three ways (not captured). Looking at changes in the bathymetry related to seafloor....

Walt Jaap: I have a question about *Lophelia pertusa*: Is there any uniqueness to the places where it is found in the Gulf that suggest that it needs protection?

Al Hine: Based on what I know on the lithoherms in the Straits of Florida, it seems they need the hard substrate. Not always have seeps but the seeps can be important for sure.

Panel 2: The Oceanographic Setting

Moderator: Kim Ritchie

Physical Oceanography in the Gulf of Mexico: Connectivity of Coastal Ecosystems and Large Scale Flows

Villy Kourafalou[1,*], George Halliwell[1], Patrick Hogan[2] and Ole-Martin Smedstad[3]
[1]Rosenstiel School of Marine and Atmospheric Science, University of Miami, Miami, FL
[2]Naval Research Lab, Stennis Space Center, MS
[3]QinetiQ North America, Technology Solutions Group – PSI, Stennis Space Center, MS

The basin-wide physical oceanographic processes in the Gulf of Mexico are dominated by the Loop Current and associated rings and eddies that not only dominate the Gulf interior, but also provide connectivity pathways among remote coastal and deep sea ecosystems. Depending on the dominant circulation conditions, various shallow and deep reefs can be connected to each other and to upstream ecosystems and neighboring sources of larvae and nutrients. For instance, coral reefs in the Northern Gulf are subject to influence from waters of low salinity and high nutrient content of river origin, mainly from the Mississippi, but also from additional rivers. Mechanisms of offshore removal of these coastal discharges that can impact the deep reefs include shelf processes (mainly wind and buoyancy driven currents), interaction with an extended Loop Current, or the presence of counter-rotating eddies in the vicinity of the river plumes. In addition, observational and numerical studies suggest that a mechanism of advection of plume waters toward the Gulf interior and toward the Straits of Florida exists, thus effectively connecting Northern and Southern Gulf of Mexico ecosystems (Ortner et al., 1995; Morey et al., 2003; Hu et al., 2005). Furthermore, the large scale current system offers connectivity pathways between ecosystems in the Gulf and the Caribbean at large.

Numerical models aid the understanding of the processes that control transport and the connectivity rates and pathways and allow the development of predictability skill that can be used in forecasting. Such an activity has been undertaken in the Rosenstiel School of Marine and Atmospheric Science of the University of Miami, in collaboration with the Naval Research Lab at Stennis Space. A regional model has been developed for the Gulf of Mexico, based on the Hybrid Coordinate Ocean Model (HYCOM) and named GoM-HYCOM. The model has a resolution of 1/25 degree (averaging ~3.5 km) and is nested within a coarser model of the entire North Atlantic, so that the larger scale current system impacting the Gulf of Mexico is well represented, while several coastal models are nested within (Kourafalou et al., 2008). Data assimilation of along track satellite altimeter observations and satellite Sea Surface Temperature (SST) retrievals directly from the orbital data is implemented through the Navy Coupled Ocean Data Assimilation scheme (NCODA, Cummings, 2005). The near real-time SST's are derived from the NOAA Advanced Very High Resolution Radiometer (AVHRR) with the use of the Multichannel Sea Surface Temperature algorithm (MCSST). The surface atmospheric forcing is provided by the three-hourly 1° horizontal resolution NOGAPS reanalysis product.

An example of fields predicted by the Regional Gulf of Mexico GoM-HYCOM model are shown in Fig. 1. The Sea Surface Height depicts the Loop Current during a phase that precedes ring shedding, along with several cyclonic and anticyclonic eddies in the basin. The Loop Current front and the eddies traveling around it are clearly seen to connect the Yucatan Strait with the Straits of Florida passing through the Northern Gulf, thus providing pathways that can connect larval spawning grounds and settlement sites, sources of nutrients or land drained pollutants and reef habitats. The Sea Surface Salinity field exhibits the interaction between the basin wide flows and the low salinity waters or river origin that dominate the Northern Gulf. The study of the complex phenomena associated with the interactions between coastal and offshore flows in the Gulf of Mexico and the ability to predict the connectivity pathways are essential components on the understanding of the ecosystem dynamics in shallow and deep reefs and the development of ecosystem based management scenarios.

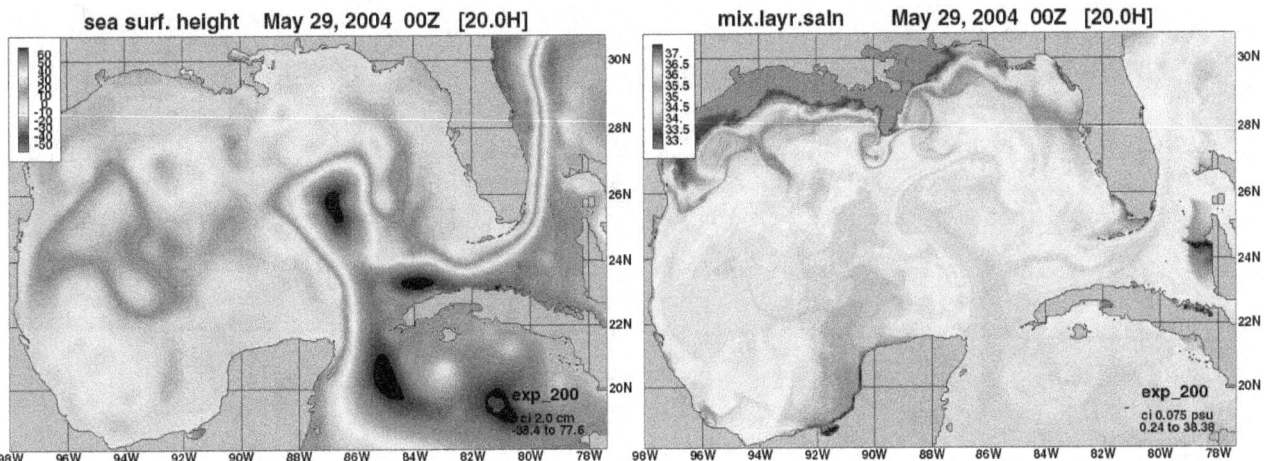

Fig. 1: Sea Surface Height (left) and sea Surface salinity (right) computed by the Gulf of Mexico Hybrid Coordinate Ocean Model (GoM-HYCOM) for May 29, 2004.

References

Cummings, J.A., 2005. Operational multivariate ocean data assimilation. *Journal of the Royal Meteorological Society,* 131, 3583 – 3604.

Hu, C. J.R. Nelson, E. Johns, Z. Chen, R. Weisberg, F. Muller-Karger, 2005. Mississippi River water in the Florida Straits and in the Gulf Stream off Georgia in summer 2004, *Geophysical Research Letters,* Vol. 32, L14606, doi:10.1029/2005GL022942.

Kourafalou V.H., G. Peng, H. Kang, P.J. Hogan, O.M. Smedstadt, R.H. Weisberg, M.O. Baringer and C.S. Meinen, 2008. Evaluation of Global Ocean Data Assimilation Experiment products on South Florida nested simulations with the Hybrid Coordinate Ocean Model. *Ocean Dynamics* (Submitted).

Morey, S.L., P.J. Martin, J.J. O'Brien, A.A. Wallcraft and J. Zavala-Hidalgo, 2003. Export pathways for river discharged fresh water in the northern Gulf of Mexico. *Journal of Geophysical Research*, 108, 3303, doi:10.1029/2002JC001674.

Ortner, P.B., T.N Lee, P.J. Milne, R.G. Zika, M.E. Clarke, G. P. Podesta, P.K. Swart, P.A. Tester, L.P. Atkinson, and W. R. Johnson, 1995. Missisippi River flood waters that reached the Gulf Stream. *Journal of Geophysical Research*, 100 (C7): 13,595-13, 601.

Coastal Ocean Circulation, Observing and Modeling Systems for the West Florida Shelf, and Applications to the 2005 Red-tide

Robert H. Weisberg

College of Marine Science, University of South Florida, St. Petersburg, FL 33701

The continental shelf is defined as the shallow, coastal ocean region linking the shoreline with the abyssal ocean. Florida has a broad, gently sloping West Florida Shelf (WFS), which receives its nutrients and other water properties through upwelling across the shelf break and communication with the major estuaries and other land drainage sources. Through such deep-ocean and estuarine interactions conditions are determined which control the ecology of the WFS, including productive recreational and commercial fisheries and blooms of *K. brevis* red tide. An underlying physical oceanographic goal is understanding the workings of the coastal ocean in uniting nutrients with light and promoting the conditions that lead to such rich ecological interactions.

To achieve this goal, the CMS-USF, in collaboration with various agencies and institutions, has developed a coordinated program of coastal ocean observing and modeling. Observations consist of: 1) moored buoys for surface meteorology, water column currents, T, S, and eventually other measures of ecological importance; 2) profiling floats and gliders for similar in-water variables; 3) HF-radar and surface drifters for surface currents; 4) and various satellite derived data products. Models consist of numerical circulation models that link the WFS with the deep-ocean and with the estuaries, along with higher resolution models of the estuaries themselves. Public domain codes are applied. The model linking the WFS with the deep-ocean is a regional adaptation of ROMS (e.g., Shchepetkin and McWilliams, 2005) nested in HYCOM (e.g., Chassignet et al., 2007); the estuarine models are adaptations of the FVCOM (Chen et al, 2003). The WFS regional model operates in an automated, nowcast/forecast mode, with results available on the internet at http://ocgweb.marine.usf.edu. Observations are also available at that web site. The FVCOM is also being used as a regional model to be nested into either ROMS or HYCOM.

A review of WFS circulation is provided by Weisberg et al. (2005). Highlights are that the Gulf of Mexico Loop Current is an important determinant of the water properties on the WFS, but that the manner in which this occurs is quite complex. For instance, remote forcing in the vicinity of the Dry Tortugas can cause upwelling onto the shelf near DeSoto Canyon followed by advection to the near shore within the bottom Ekman layer. This, along with anomalous upwelling favorable winds, accounted for the high nutrient and primary productivity states in 1998 (Weisberg et al., 2003 and Walsh et al., 2003). Such interannual variability greatly affects the ecology of the WFS. Seasonal variability is also documented, with a fairly regular annual cycle of preferentially upwelling circulation in fall through spring months, versus downwelling circulation in summer months. Whereas the Loop Current impacts the WFS, it is isolated from the shelf itself via the Taylor-Proudman theorem (He and Weisberg, 2003).
Other recent accomplishments include the characterization of the 2005 red tide bloom through advection from offshore to the near shore region, again via the bottom Ekman layer. We used the regional ROMS/HYCOM model formulation to demonstrate these pathways and to account for the evolution of the red tide observations. We also demonstrated, using profiling floats along

with the model, the origin of water that led to strong stratification and the associated benthic die-off that occurred during the 2005 red tide event, and on the basis of these successes we initiated a red-tide tracking tool in the model. An outgrowth of these activities is a new, Center for Prediction of Red tide (CPR) joint between USF and the FWC. CPR will be coupling the physical with biological models and intends to advance the predictive capabilities of these coupled models through data assimilation.

Some additional lessons learned are that long time series are essential in describing the workings of the WFS circulation. We are attempting to acquire these through the maintenance of a coastal ocean observing system. Observations alone, however, are insufficient, and models alone are fraught with error. It is through the close coordination of these two activities that advancements in understanding and prediction of ecologically important processes on the WFS will be achieved.

References

Chassignet, E. P., Hurlburt, H. E., Smedstad, O. M., Halliwell, G. R., Hogan, P. J., Wallcraft, A. J., Baraille, R., Bleck, R. (2007). The HYCOM (Hybrid Coordinate Ocean Model) Data Assimilative System. Journal of Marine Systems 65 (1-4), 60–83.

Chen, C., H. Liu, and R.C. Beardsley. 2003. An unstructured grid, finite volume, three-dimensional, primitive equations ocean model: Applications to coastal ocean and estuaries. *J. Atm. Ocean Tech.*, 20, 159-186.

He, R and R.H. Weisberg (2003). A Loop Current intrusion case study on the West Florida Shelf. *J.Phys. Oceanogr.*, 33, 465-477.

Shchepetkin, A. and J. McWilliams (2005). The Regional Oceanic Modeling System: A split-explicit, free-surface, topography-following-coordinate ocean model. *Ocean Modelling*, 9, 347–404.

Walsh, J.J., R.H. Weisberg, D.A. Dieterle, R. He, B.P. Darrow, J.K. Jolliff, K.M. Lester, G.A. Vargo, G.J. Kirkpatrick, K.A. Fanning, T.T. Sutton, A.E. Jochens, D.C. Briggs, B. Nababan, C. Hu, and F. Muller-Karger (2003). The phytoplankton response to intrusions of slope water on the West Florida Shelf: models and observations. *J. Geophys. Res.*, 108, C6, 21, doi:10.1029/2002JC001406.

Weisberg, R.H. and R. He (2003). Local and deep-ocean forcing contributions to anomalous water properties on the West Florida Shelf. *J. Geophys. Res.,* 108, C6, 15, doi:10.1029/2002JC001407.

Weisberg, R.H., R. He, Y. Liu, and J.I. Virmani (2005). West Florida shelf circulation on synoptic, seasonal, and inter-annual time scales, in Circulation in the Gulf of Mexico, W. Sturges and A. Lugo-Fernandez, eds., AGU monograph series, Geophysical Monograph 161, 325-347.

Panel 2 Discussion

Villy Kourafalou (University of Miami/RSMAS) –presentation/ panelist
Bob Weisberg (University of South Florida College of Marine Science) – presentation/panelist
Libby Johns (NOAA Atlantic Oceanographic & Meteorological Lab) –panelist
Liz Williams (University of Miami/RSMAS) - panelist

(from meeting transcripts)

Andy Shepard: Are internal waves a factor we need to think about as well?

Bob Weisberg: Yes, I think all these models have to be complete enough. Most of the models probably don't account for what you are talking about. They may not have the internal waves in them, but if they can get the stratification right, they probably are capturing them.

Jerry Ault: What about the contribution of the Cuban Shelf that is huge and has many of the same species?

Villy Kourafalou: Quite a few studies have been done - some with collaborations with Cuba – looking at how larvae would be entrained and carried across. We went to Cuba for a conference a few years ago – but it was very difficult for people to get visas, etc. Depending on the position of the Florida current, I don't think that north Cuba would be much of a source. More collaboration would be needed. South Cuba models show connections to loop currents. Loop current provides connectivity.

John Ogden: To what extent does existing understanding of oceanography demonstrate that these areas are linked and are there knowledge gaps identified?

Bob Weisberg: It is clear that we don't have a good handle on what determines a loop current shedding event. The loop current is what provides the connectivity. The whole process of loop current penetration into the Gulf of Mexico, the maintenance of the Gulf of Mexico and the eventually shedding the eddies is a major gap. Every year is unique – there are long term secular variations. In recent years the loop current has penetrated farther into the Gulf of Mexico and has sustained for longer and we don't understand why.

Villy Kourafalou: One of the main problems is the type of data that go in to the models. There is a lot of information that we use for the models, but that isn't necessarily good enough. There are no profiles in terms of what is happening underneath the surface – we need that information. Doing some work to find out where the gaps are that would be most important.

Bob Weisberg: We have these different habitats, and we'd like to know if they are connected. There is a geological basis for connection. But what makes them a suitable habitat. And for that, circulation has to play a role. These are the questions that we have to address? It may not be as simple as Islands in the Stream.

Gene Shinn: Regardless of what the models say, there has to be some connectivity given all the studies that have been done showing direct connectivity.

Libby Johns: I am going to talk later today about some new, direct data that show that the models are correct.

Steve Altran: How much bottom data systems to we have compared to the surface and are we attempting to get more coverage?

Bob Weisberg: Very few are getting information on the water column at all. Until recently there haven't been in water sensors on the NOAA buoys. Most of the work on that has been by academics. Your observation is a good one.

Paul Sammarco: Should be interesting to meld data on circulation patterns and coral genetics. Eleven species of tropical corals are on oil platforms. Molecular data (have been/are being) collected to study genetic relationships of these corals.

Ian MacDonald: High temperature and lower pH are two stressors on corals – are there models to predict the effects of those on corals?

Bob Weisberg: I haven't seen a compelling change in temperature from my geological colleagues. pH may be another story.

Libby Johns: Jim Hendee has been working on temperature plus UV really correlates with how well the coral reefs are doing.

Paul Sammarco: Large scale eddies – don't tend to shift onto the shelf – is it possible to get the top of the eddy to get wind sheared onto the shelf?

Bob Weisberg: It occurs on a pressure scale – can have penetration on a certain scale. You can get deep water properties permeating across the shelf. It draws down to a matter of scale.

I want to make one comment on connectivity – obviously there is connectivity. The issue of larval recruitment: there is a lot of inter annual variability. We have to look at the details of it, not the generalities.

Liz Williams: There are also wind events – where you have a southwest wind impinging on the topography. Not just the eddies, it's also the wind events interact with coastal waters.

Panel 3: Benthic Characterizations

Moderator: Brian Keller

Gulf of Mexico Initiative
Northwestern Gulf of Mexico

Emma L. Hickerson and G.P. Schmahl
Flower Garden Banks National Marine Sanctuary, Galveston TX

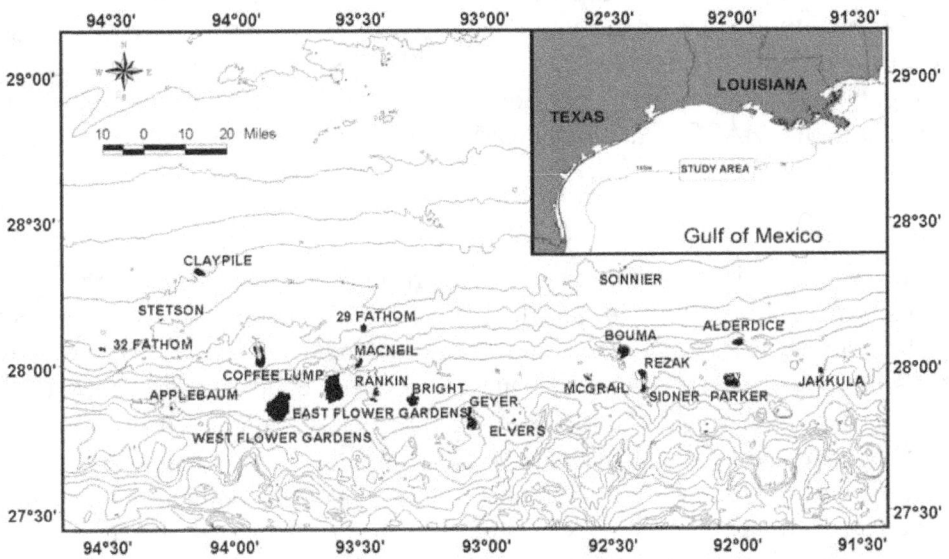

The reefs and banks of the northwestern Gulf of Mexico have been the focus of investigations by the research team from the Flower Garden Banks National Marine Sanctuary for the past ten years. Since 1997, collaborative efforts between NOAA, USGS, and the University of New Hampshire have resulted in the collection of close to 4000 square kilometers (1525 sq. miles) of high-resolution multibeam bathymetry, detailing thirteen different banks, and some areas connecting various locations.

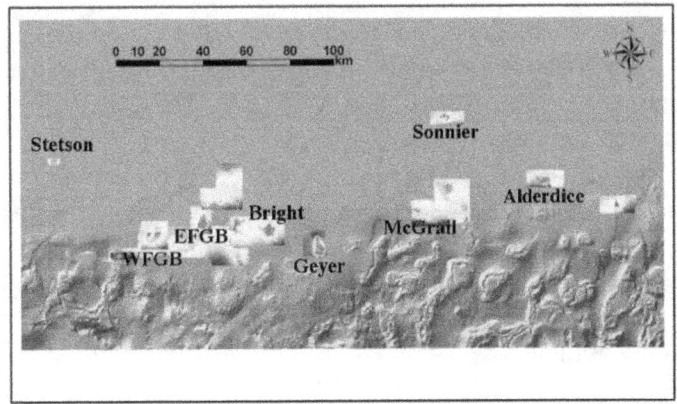

Various levels of management and protection are in place in this region. The East and West Flower Gardens and Stetson Banks are the three areas within the Flower Garden Banks National Marine Sanctuary (FGBNMS), and carry a Sanctuary protection through Sanctuary regulations. Anchoring is illegal throughout the Sanctuary through the International Maritime Organization No Anchor Regulations. Commercial and recreational hook and line fishing are allowed. There is an active gas platform, HIA389A, within the boundaries of the Sanctuary, at East Flower Garden Bank. All reefs and banks in the region are protected from direct impacts from oil and gas activities through regulations placed on the industry through Minerals Management Service (MMS). The following banks are designated as Habitat Areas of Particular Concern (HAPC's) by NOAA Fisheries: Stetson, East and West FGB, MacNeil, 29 Fathom, Rankin, 29 Fathom, Bright, Geyer, Sonnier, McGrail, Bouma, Rezak, Sidner, Alderdice, and Jakkula. This designation does not carry any protective regulations in itself, however, when fisheries of species are evaluated, these areas must be taken into consideration. Three of these locations do carry regulations as part of the HAPC designation, due to the presence of coral reefs: East and West FGB, and McGrail Bank. At the request of the FGBNMS, Stetson Bank was also afforded the additional regulatory requirements.   The following activities are prohibited by fishing vessels through this additional HAPC regulatory measures: bottom longline, bottom trawl, buoy gear, dredge, pot, or trap, and bottom anchoring.

The earliest explorations of the Flower Garden Banks were led by Dr. Thomas Pulley, then Director Emeritus of the Houston Museum of Natural Science, during the early 1960's. These investigations continued under the auspices of Flower Gardens Ocean Research Center (FGORC), founded by Robert Alderdice and James Covington in the late 1960's. Texas A&M University led the science expeditions during the 1970's, under the guidance of researchers including Drs. Thomas Bright, Richard Rezak, and David McGrail. Their investigations, funded primarily by the Bureau of Land Management, (BLM), now Minerals Management Service (MMS) covered the geographic area of the northwestern Gulf of Mexico, and was driven for the need to characterize the reefs and banks in the face of advancing oil and gas exploration and extraction activities. Their efforts resulted in volumes of BLM reports covering oceanography, geology, and biology of features in the Northwestern Gulf of Mexico. A comprehensive book entitled Reefs and Banks of the Northwestern Gulf of Mexico continues to be an outstanding reference for this region (Rezak et al. 1985). One of the outcomes of this research era was the development of Ecological Zonation description of each of the reefs and banks based on their observations to each of the banks. This exceptional wealth of baseline information has guided the current investigations by the Flower Garden Banks research team.

Since 1998, the Flower Garden Banks NMS has led twelve expeditions to further characterize the reefs and banks of the Northwestern Gulf of Mexico, building upon the knowledge gained by the early investigations by Bright, Rezak, and McGrail. These expeditions have utilized both manned submersibles and remotely operated vehicles (ROV's). These cruises have resulted in over 218 hours of survey time, 177 ROV surveys, the collection of approximately 250 directed samples, and the collection of close to 8500 high resolution digital still images. The majority of the surveys have taken place within the boundaries of the FGBNMS, however some surveys have been conducted at other NW GOM locations: Bright (3 surveys), Sonnier (1 survey), McGrail (20 surveys), Alderdice (3 surveys), Pinnacles (5 surveys). The surveys typically ranged between 50m to 150m depth.

Real time annotations of the ROV surveys were produced for the majority of the ROV surveys, detailing fish species and number estimates, benthic community, and geology. An inventory of the biology in all of the digital still images has been developed – all of the images are georeferenced, so can be visualized through GIS applications.

A series of reference posters have been developed, depicting the major biological components encountered during the surveys – antipatharians, octocorals, fishes, sponges, and algae and invertebrates. Many of the images used in the posters were taken of samples *in situ*, prior to collection. Taxonomy experts are collaborating with the FGBNMS to identify the samples. In many cases when high resolution images of the biology were provided to experts, identification was not possible due to the fact that the taxonomists had only seen preserved specimens. This is the reason behind the development of the posters depicting the *in situ* organisms before they become specimens to be identified. We believe that these posters can be useful reference material on a regional level. High resolution versions of the posters can be downloaded at: http://flowergarden.noaa.gov/document_library/sci_documents.html. Some of the specimens are yet to be identified.

The surveys have prompted the FGBNMS to update the Biological Habitat Classification Scheme, based on higher resolution capabilities, sampling, and observations. A workshop was held to assist in guiding this effort. Biological Habitat Classification Maps for the East and West Flower Garden Banks and Stetson Bank were developed, based on the updated Classification Scheme. This updated scheme is presented in the 2008 releases of the publications, Coral Reefs of the U.S.A, and in the State of Coral Reef Ecosystems of the Flower Garden Banks, Stetson Bank, and Other Banks in the Northwestern Gulf of Mexico, which is a section in the State of the Coral Reef Ecosystems of the United States and Pacific Freely Associated States: 2008. We feel that the updated scheme is applicable in all of the outer and mid-shelf reefs and banks in the Northwestern Gulf of Mexico.

Of note is the updated information pertaining to McGrail Bank, which contains a unique *Stephanocoenia intersepta* coral reef. This reef was granted regulatory protection through the HAPC designation, and was featured in a paper by Schmahl and Hickerson (2006). Approximately 28% coral cover was measured during ROV surveys in areas dominated by large *Stephanocoenia* colonies – upwards of 3-4m across.

Limited surveys have also been conducted at the Alabama/Mississippi Pinnacles area by the FGBNMS research team. High resolution multibeam bathymetric data was obtained in 2000 by Dr. J. Gardner (University of New Hampshire), in cooperation with USGS. http://walrus.wr.usgs.gov/pacmaps/pn-index.html. Minerals Management Service have funded several investigations targeting this region.

The Flower Garden Banks is currently undergoing a review of the Sanctuary Management Plan. The top issues identified through the public scoping process were boundary expansion, fishing impacts, visitor use, water quality, education/outreach, and enforcement. A ranking process was undertaken for the boundary expansion issue, and a list of locations were submitted to the FGBNMS by the Sanctuary Advisory Council (SAC) to move forward through a boundary expansion process. The recommendation by the SAC was to adjust the boundaries for Stetson

Bank and East and West Flower Garden Banks, to better encompass the existing biological and geological features, and to expand the boundaries to encompass the following banks: Horseshoe, MacNeil, Rankin, 28 Fathom, Bright, Geyer, Sonnier, Alderdice, and McGrail Banks. The FGBNMS is in the process of drafting the EIS for these areas. In addition to the boundary expansion activities, the SAC recommended that the FGBNMS conduct an Experimental Research Closure to assess the affects of fishing and diving at the FGBNMS. A Research Closure Workshop is scheduled to be held in April, 2008, to design the closure and subsequent monitoring.

The FGBNMS acknowledges the following people who have contributed their time, ideas, expertise, and encouragement for the research conducted in deepwater habitat of the Northwestern Gulf of Mexico since 1998:

Dr. Sylvia Earle (National Geographic, DOER Marine, Inc.)
Dr. Jim Gardner (University of New Hampshire, formerly USGS)
Lance Horn (NURC-UNCW)
Steve Cairns (Smithsonian Insitute)
Dennis Opresko (Smithsonian Institute)
Klaus Ruetzler (Smithsonian Institute)
Mary Wicksten (Texas A&M University)
Doug Weaver (Texas A&M University – Corpus Christi, formerly FGBNMS)

Absent from these acknowledgements is an extensive list of collaborators who have participated in the cruises, and assisted with identification of specimens.

References

Rezak, R., T.J. Bright, and D.W. McGrail. 1985. Reefs and Banks of the Northwestern Gulf of Mexico: Their Geological, Biological, and Physical Dynamics. John Wiley and Sons, New York, 259 pp.

Schmahl, GP and EL Hickerson. 2006. McGrail Bank, a deep tropical coral reef community in the northwestern Gulf of Mexico. Proceedings of the 10th International Coral Reef Symposium, 1124-1130. Japanese Coral Reef Society, Tokyo, Japan.

Long-Term Reef Monitoring at the Flower Garden Banks:
Status, Stasis and Change

W.F. Precht[1], R.B. Aronson[2], K.J.P. Deslarzes[3], L.S. Kaufman[4],
M.L. Robbart[5], E.L. Hickerson[6], G.P. Schmahl[6], J. Sinclair[7]

[1]Battelle Memorial Institute, Miami FL
[2]Dauphin Island Sea Lab, Dauphin Island, AL
[3]Geo-Marine, Inc. New Iberia, LA
[4]Biology Department, Boston University, Boston, MA
[5]Dial-Cordy & Associates Inc.
[6]Flower Garden Banks National Marine Sanctuary, Galveston, TX
[7]Gulf of Mexico Region, Minerals Management Service, Metairie, LA

History

The coral reefs of the Flower Garden Banks (FGB) are among the most sensitive biological communities in U.S. federal waters of the Gulf of Mexico. In 1973, the Minerals Management Service (MMS) established a program of protective activities at those reefs. Two sites, each 100 m x 100 m and 17–26 m deep, have been monitored since 1988: one on the East Bank and the other on the West Bank. MMS has been monitoring these sites on a long-term basis to detect any changes caused by oil and gas activities.

The current monitoring effort represents a whole-ecosystem approach to assessing these sensitive and valuable coral-reef resources. Included in the monitoring program are: (1) assessments of water quality; (2) fish and sea-urchin surveys; (3) benthic surveys from videotapes of randomly located, 10-m transects; (4) surveys of coral populations in repetitively photographed, 8-m^2 quadrats; (5) quantification of lateral growth of individual colonies of the brain coral *Diploria strigosa*; and (6) sclerochronology of cores taken from colonies of *Montastraea faveolata*. These measures provide an integrated picture of stability and incipient change at the FGB. The salient results presented here help explain, largely by counterexample, the rampant degradation of reef ecosystems observed in the wider Caribbean region over the last few decades.

Current Status

Monitoring results for 2002-2006 highlighted the continued health of these reefs, expressed as consistently high coral cover, ranging from 50% coral cover to 64%. These results are consistent with past monitoring results showing no decline since coral cover was first monitored at the FGB in 1978–82. The *Montastraea annularis* complex persists as the dominant species complex from 2002-2006 (27%-40%), and *Diploria strigosa* (3%-13%) continues to be the second most prevalent species at both banks. Other coral species are represented at the East and West Banks, including *Porites astreoides* (3%-8%) and *Montastraea cavernosa* (2%-8%). After these top four coral species, ten species make up the remainder of coral cover within the random transects (Precht et al. 2006; Precht et al. in press).

Macroalgae ranged from 4% to 34% from 2002-2006, with a high occurring at the East Bank in 2005. It should be noted that in 2005 and 2006 monitoring took place in June, while past monitoring events took place in the fall months (September-November). Seasonal variation in macroalgal populations is well documented. From 2002-2004 macroalgal cover ranged from 4%-19% across both banks and from 2005-2006 macroalgal cover ranged from 13% to 34%. When comparing macroalgae estimates between banks, West Bank results were consistently lower than East Bank values from 2003, 2005, and 2006.

Crustose coralline, turf and bare space (CTB) showed a reciprocal relationship with macroalgae in all years at both banks. Between 2002 and 2006, CTB ranged from 12%-37%, with the low occurring at the East Bank in 2005 and the high at the East Bank in 2002. CTB was higher at the West Bank than at the East Bank from 2003-2006. These complementary fluctuations were probably generated by differences in the time of sampling in 2004 (fall) as compared to 2005 (spring). Sea urchins occurred at low densities as in the past, and herbivorous fishes continued at high densities compared to Caribbean reefs that are heavily fished.

The tight, reciprocal relationship between macroalgae and CTB at the FGB, in the absence of any complementary fluctuation in coral cover, highlights the control that coral cover exerts on the cover of other benthic components. The balance of coral growth, recruitment and mortality determines the availability of space for algal growth. At the FGB, continuing low levels of coral mortality result in persistently high coral cover. Short-term fluctuations in the balance between macroalgae and CTB are secondarily driven by seasonal changes in water temperature, and possibly also by transient fluctuations in herbivory and other factors.

The Role of Hurricanes, Bleaching and Disease

New threats to coral populations at the FGB from bleaching, hurricanes and disease could drive those reefs in the direction of lower coral cover and higher macroalgal cover, which would make them increasingly similar to Caribbean reefs. As Aronson et al. (2005) noted "The high coral cover of reefs at the FGB contrasts markedly with the degraded state of reefs throughout the southern Gulf of Mexico, Florida, the Bahamas and the Caribbean." However, in that same paper it was noted, "due to ... the recent occurrence of hurricanes and bleaching events, these coral reef ecosystems could change in the future." Dismally, these words would prove prophetic within the same year.

Hurricane Rita made landfall on the Texas/Louisiana coast on 24 September 2005. The storm's track took the eye to within 48 km of the East Flower Garden Bank. Waves were projected to be as high as 18 meters (m) in advance of the storm for the FGB, and sustained wave heights of 5 to 6 m for almost 24 hours were recorded at the closest monitoring buoy some 153 km due west of the West Bank (and well west of the storm track). Hurricane Rita was a Category 5 hurricane on the Saffir-Simpson Scale with sustained winds of 140 mph prior to approaching the Gulf of Mexico shelf break on Friday, 23 September.

While there have been a number of small hurricanes to pass within 100 miles of these topographic features in recent years, Hurricane Rita was the first major hurricane (Category 3 or larger) to pass over (within 80 kilometers [km]) the reefs of the Flower Garden Banks (FGB) since the passage of Hurricane Allen in 1980 (Alexis-Lugo personal communication). Hurricane Allen, a Category 5 storm, is known to have caused localized physical impacts such as displacing Volkswagen-size reef substrate and coral heads (up to two tons in weight) on the reef cap of the FGB. Unfortunately, the continuous, long-term monitoring effort of MMS and NOAA at the FGB was not ongoing at the time, so most of the reports of reef damage from that storm are purely anecdotal.

Sanctuary personnel made it out to the reefs approximately two weeks after the passing of the hurricane to document the effects of the storm. Large colonies of coral and pieces of reef rock with many corals had been plucked out the reef, overturned, and tossed around. The wave energy must have been quite significant as about meter of sand had been scoured out from the sand flats. Large barrel sponges had been "topped," and those that were close to sand patches and survived the storm were filled with sand. Although random transect data was not taken during a post-hurricane assessment data collection cruise in November 2005, random transect data was taken in June 2006. June 2006 random transect data revealed high CTB levels at East and West Bank (23% and 25%). Unexpectedly, macroalgae showed disparate patterns at East (21%) and West Bank (13%) in 2006.

Coral cover and changes in community structure were measured in November 2005 using repetitive quadrat images and perimeter video at the East Bank long-term monitoring site. Hurricane waves were responsible for overturning large coral colonies, scouring, gouging, and the removal of sand from sand flats, as well as bending stainless steel rods on the reef cap (65-75 FSW). Although there were dramatic effects of the hurricane at the East Bank, coral cover was not appreciably affected according to repetitive quadrat results. 2% of coral colonies were missing in the 40 repetitive quadrat photographs taken on the coral cap (70-85 FSW), while only 0.5% of colonies were missing at 9 deep repetitive quadrat stations (105-131 FSW). Levels of coral bleaching were relatively high for the FGB (~6% on the coral cap), but bleaching had been observed before the hurricane (NOAA cruise August 23-27), and it is not known whether the hurricane exacerbated bleaching or whether it may have brought relief in the form of cooler water temperatures. Water quality data results showed that the passage of Hurricane Rita brought cooler water temperatures to the banks after 50 days of elevated temperatures.

In addition, during the early months of 2005, researchers were alarmed to find widespread plague-like coral disease affecting multiple colonies and multiple species, reef wide. This was the first time on record of such an occurrence of this magnitude at this site. It was an unusual event, as typically, coral disease strikes during the warmer, summer months whereas this outbreak occurred during the winter months. As the summer of 2005 progressed and water temperatures increased, the corals started to expel their zooxanthellae, which are symbiotic algae that live in the coral tissues and provide the coral with nutrition through the process of photosynthesis. By October, approximately 45% of the colonies of the corals on the coral cap, down to a 29 m water depth, or so, were affected by bleaching to some extent. This was the worst coral bleaching event on record at the FGB. Initial observations in mid-October, 2005, indicated between 35% and 40% of the colonies were bleached to some extent - partially or fully. The bleaching appeared to be affecting 100% of the fire coral (*Millepora alcicornis*) and great star coral (*Montastraea cavernosa*), and affecting at least eleven other species to varying degrees. In follow-up surveys conducted in March 2006, approximately 4% to 5% of the coral colonies still exhibited various levels of bleaching. By June 2006 the bleaching event was over. Analysis is ongoing to document the level of coral mortality associated with this event.

Despite the hardships placed on the coral reef during 2005, the corals mostly recovered from the 2005 disease event, although a second event was documented during the winter months of 2006. As the waters warmed, the progress of the disease slowed down. The reef recovered from the severe bleaching event, although it is suspected that a substantial amount of fire coral was lost. In August and September 2006, as testament to the resiliency of the reef, two spectacular spawning events took place—new life begins. Unfortunately, future disease, bleaching, and hurricane events may not be so easily overcome and survived.

Recent Discoveries

The first living colonies of *Acropora palmata* were discovered on the FGB in 2003 and 2005 (Zimmer et al. 2005). Those discoveries, coupled with a known history of bank flooding since the last glacial maximum, led our team to predict that *Acropora*-dominated reefs underlie and form the structural foundation of the living reef community at the FGB. In June 2006, while Precht and Deslarzes were scuba diving on the southeast corner of the East FGB, they examined an open cave at 21 m depth, which exposed a 3-m vertical section of the reef subsurface just below the living community. Within that exposure we discovered large branches and trunks of *A. palmata* (>1 m in height) in growth position. Radiocarbon dating of a branch from a colony at the top of the section yielded a conventional date of 6330 ± 60 ^{14}Cyr (radiocarbon years before 1950), corresponding to a calibrated age of 6780 calbp. Follow-up surveys by our team in June 2007 revealed an *A. palmata* dominated under story dating between 10-6 thousand years on both banks. The discovery of fossil *Acropora* has profound implications for understanding the history of reef development at the FGB. The banks supported a shallow, warm-water, reef-coral assemblage up until ~6000 years ago. This community lagged behind rapidly rising sea level in the middle Holocene. As sea temperatures cooled in the late Holocene the reef was capped by a temperature variable deeper-water assemblage dominated by massive corals, which persists to this day.

During our 2007 surveys our team also found the first fossils of *Acropora cervicornis* on the East FGB. This species appears to have persisted until the Little Ice Age in deeper water on the flanks of the Bank. Follow-up studies are proposed to document and explain the turn-on and turn-off mechanisms through time and space for *Acropora* reef development on these isolated reef complexes.

Pulley Ridge

Walter C. Jaap[1] and Robert Halley[2]

[1]Present address: Florida Institute of Oceanography, St. Petersburg FL
[2]US Geological Survey, St. Petersburg, FL

Pulley Ridge (eastern Gulf of Mexico) is composed of coastal carbonate deposits; it is approximately 300 km long (24° 40'N to 26° 40' N), north-south alignment, width is up to 15 km wide; depth ranges from 60 to 90 m. It was named in the 1950s after the famous malacologist E.T. Pulley. Recent expeditions to the area employing modern seismic tools, ROVs, submersibles, towed camera sleds, and mixed gas diving has revealed a unique reef system. The southernmost 30 km is a drowned barrier island, including dunes, spits, tidal inlets, and cat's eye ponds. The island became a submerged shoal following rising sea level caused by glacial melting. After flooding, the shoal was colonized by corals and other reef organisms. Seismic data indicate that the coral structure atop the shoal is 1 to 2 m thick, formed at about 6 to 14 thousand years ago; vertical growth rate is estimated at 14 cm/thousand years (see Jarrett et al., Strange bedfellows – a deep hermatypic coral reef superimposed on a drowned barrier island; southern Pulley Ridge, SW Florida platform margin. Mar Geol 214 (2005): 295–307).

Although the southern portion of Pulley Ridge is a somewhat unique coral reef system, there are similarities to deeper (>60 m) reefs and banks in Jamaica, Bahamas, Belize, and off Texas. Autotrophic organisms (coralline and green algae, and zooxanthellate corals) are very common in the southern 30 km of Pulley Ridge, while to the north, it is composed of rocky outcrops colonized by heterotrophic organisms (sponges, octocorals, azooxanthellate solitary and colonial Scleractinia, and crinoids). The southern area is considered the deepest zooxanthellate coral reef on the continental shelf of North America. Photosynthetic Active Radiation (PAR) reaching the reef was 5 to 30 microEinsteins/m^2 sec^{-1}; one to five percent of the surface PAR. In this very low illumination, autotrophic organisms flourish including several species of crustose coralline algae encrusting rocks and gravel plus the leafy green alga (*Anadyomene menziesii*). This alga was very abundant during DeepWorker submersible investigations. The sunray lettuce coral

(*Leptoseris cucullata*) is the most commonly seen of the zooxanthellate Scleractinia. In many cases the reef structure is composed of multiple layers of *L. cucullata* and other lettuce coral species (genus *Agaricia*), it resembles stacks of potato chips. Coral laminations are loosely connected and easily moved; we observed grouper, moving the stack to find refuge. There are at least seven species of zooxanthellate Scleractinia on Pulley Ridge. Cover analysis based on 1000 photos from 14 towed SeaBoss photo transects reported that coralline algae contributed 5 to 43% of benthic cover, the green alga *Anadyomene menziesii* provided 0.3 to 24% of cover, and zooxanthellate Scleractinia (mostly Agariciidae) were responsible for 0 to 23% of cover (Hine et al., Coral Reefs, Present and Past, on the West Florida Shelf and Platform Margin, in press, Springer, in United States Coral Reefs).

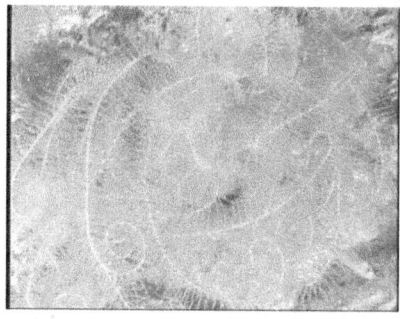

As previously mentioned, the vast majority of Pulley Ridge is composed of rock features, some with steep escarpment faces that suggest they were formed by erosion. There are numerous undercut ledges typical of the eastern Gulf of Mexico shallow hard bottom communities. These ledges and depression features provide refuges for fish. The tops of the ridge are colonized by Ellisellid and and Nicellid octocorals (sea fans and sea plumes). The ledge promontories had moderately strong bottom currents. We observed that the down current sides of the structures attracted multitudes of small fish and attached invertebrates that were foraging on the plankton carried in the currents. Sponges, crinoids, azooxanthellate solitary Scleractinia were sparsely distributed on the rocky horizontal surfaces. *Oculina tennela* (an azooxanthellate colonial scleractinian coral) was moderately common as were stylasterine hydrocorals.

Pulley Ridge is a significant commercial fishing area. Grouper, snapper, and amberjack are the focus of this fishing. The reef structure and resident fauna provide refuge and food for higher trophic level fish. There are approximately 90 species of fish; shallow and deep reef species are represented in the fauna.

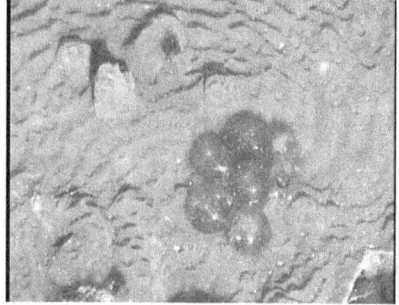

Pulley Ridge has not suffered from major disturbances either natural or anthropogenic. The remoteness and depth offer natural protection. Southern Pulley Ridge reef is susceptible to degradation due to its fragile structure. If illegal anchoring, traps, or trawls were used on the southern reef area, the structure would collapse. Because of the extremely low levels of light and coincident reef growth rates, recovery would be very slow.

Panel 3 Discussion

Emma Hickerson (NOAA Flower Garden Banks NMS) – presentation/panelist
Bill Precht (Battelle, Inc.) – presentation/panelist
Walt Jaap (present address: Florida Institute of Oceanography) – presentation/panelist

Billy Causey: The boundary between a more subtropical and tropical environment – you have a greater number of species because you have both tropical and subtropical species. Would you agree with that kind of assessment? Do you see Pulley Ridge as a healthy area?

Walt Jaap: The Pulley Ridge area and the Florida Middle Grounds area are healthy. The complexities of the system where the Tortugas are located make it a nice settling ground. The temperate areas are important.

Letise Houser: How well are the corals recovering from the "triple punch"? How well do you think the introduced coral might thrive or how will it impact the structure of the system?

Bill Precht: With the triple punch, while there was mortality from the hurricane; the bleaching had little impact on mortality. The disease event stopped when the temperatures went up. So some of that has recovered. The numbers seem to be staying the same in terms of coral cover. The reefs still look really good. As far as the *Acropora* – there seem to be range expansions of the *Acropora* species. Interesting about FGB – one of the reasons the coral cover is so high, the other reefs in the Caribbean were dominated by the *Acropora* species. So one of the reasons the coral cover at the Flower Gardens was so high is that they didn't have the *Acropora*. If the *Acropora* starts dominating in the FGB and then is ephemeral due to these other diseases, it could result in less coral cover.

Emma Hickerson: Regarding bleaching at Stetson, which is dominated by *Millepora*. We did see a loss of coral cover there. We are seeing some recovery, but there was loss. Regarding the disease – it affected 7 species. The first major event was in 2005. But we've seen it since in 2006 & 2007 as well, but not as significant. If it continues to peck away at the reef every winter, it may lead to declines over time. The Flower Garden Banks has prolific spawning events. We haven't seen a significant drop in spawning since these events.

Andy Shepard: One of the functions of a network of areas would be to sustain productivity. Again – how does the network look? Are there other areas?

Walt Jaap: It looks good for the eastern gulf. Might consider one of the *Lophelia* areas because there is a lot of research being done with *Lophelia*. Don't know if there are separate species or not. Between the Florida Middle Grounds and Pulley Ridge there are some nice hard bottom habitat. You might want to consider one of them. Maybe one of the old Hourglass stations would be good.

Emma Hickerson: We haven't talked about the South Texas Banks. Wes Tunnell is here and can talk about that. In the Flower Garden Banks & the NW Gulfs we've gone through a ranking system and some of the banks didn't make the list because we didn't have the information and we need to put more effort into understanding.

Villy Kourafalou: Are there data available on some of these locations and is there data on the correlation between what you see on these reefs (freshwater)

+ We have cores thru coral heads and look at signatures from terrestrial runoff. The question is: does that have impacts on the reef in a negative way? Does any of that runoff when combined with bleaching, does that make the corals more susceptible, did it increase the bleaching event or decrease? These things raise more questions than we have answers. Also, we have to have by off from the Mexicans for this. There are no shallow reef communities in the Gulf. They are getting larvae from Mexico or Cuba or other places. Have to have other areas part of this – talking about involving Mexico.

Walt Jaap: There was an event in 1977 that extirpated everything. The community was still like that a few years ago.

Paul Sammarco: What are the temperatures like at Pulley Ridge?

Walt Jaap: Similar to what you see in Tortugas Bank – 29 or 30 degrees in the summer maybe down to 23 degrees in the winter.

Bob Weisberg: Is there seasonality in the corals?

Walt Jaap: There is a spawning event in September and October. Some of the other corals may be doing it more frequently.

Emma Hickerson: At the Flower Garden Banks we are dominated by *Montastraea* species; The majority of live cover are mass spawning species. The timing of spawning here is very predictable: 7-10 days after the full moon in September. This is an extremely prolific event.

Julie Morris: Can you talk more about the importance of the hard bottoms of the West Florida Shelf?

Walt Jaap: Very significant area. One graduate student is looking at recovery from the red tide from a few years ago. Taken 1-2 years to see the recovery of coral recruitment. The hard bottom communities in the eastern gulf are islands separated by sediment areas; somewhat ephemeral – getting covered by sediments. Recommend that hourglass series of taxonomic studies in the eastern gulf.

Panel 4: Fish and Fisheries Characterization/ Spawning Aggregations

Moderator: Kim Ritchie

Fish and Fisheries in the Gulf of Mexico

Jerald Ault

University of Miami, Rosenstiel School of Marine and Atmospheric Science, Miami, FL

In assessing the potential to reach the goal of sustaining key regional fisheries in the context of the '*Islands in the* Stream' initiative, it is incumbent upon us to evaluate whether there are appropriate data and a conceptual framework adequate for the mission that we have in mind?

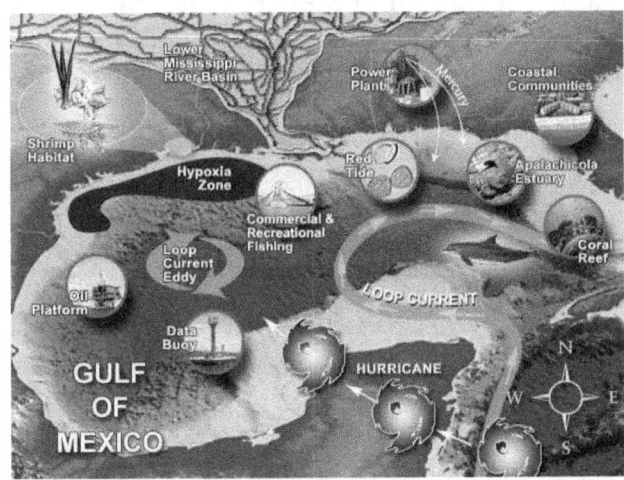

The Gulf of Mexico fishery ecosystem spans a wide range of habitats and biogeographical environments, from tropical to subtropical marine in the south, to temperate-estuarine in the north. These environments are connected by the very energetic physical oceanographic current systems that regulate the biological and fisheries productivity of the ecosystem. The fisheries of the Gulf of Mexico are greatly influenced by exploitation, habitat degradation, hurricanes and pollution. To sustain these economically- and ecologically-important resources, it is critical that we develop a system science perspective when tackling such an enormous and complex problem. This would entail linking the dynamics of the ocean environment with range of uses and drivers of systems productivity. The goal would be to develop an integrated information management system that successfully links assimilation of key data on population dynamics, habitats and bioeconomics to a range of model-building activities that link fisheries biology, ocean physics, habitats and humans, which would provide the basis for fishery resource risk assessments to policy alternatives. This will be a challenge, because for many important resources data have not been collected until very recently, limiting our understanding of what were the historical limits of ecosystem productivity.

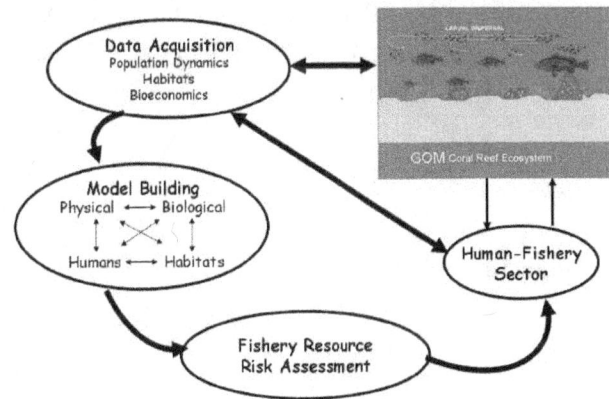

Designing Marine Reserves for Fishery Management

A very important forward-looking component of monitoring, data assimilation and modeling are maps of the resources to ocean environments. In the Florida Keys we have relatively good maps that define habitats, circulation dynamics, bathymetry and rugosity, for example, but a major limitation is that not all areas are mapped. For example, the West Florida shelf is not well mapped. This will have to be a priority mission as the GOM IITS initiative moves forward.

The economics and ecology of the Gulf of Mexico have been historically dominated by large commercial fishery enterprises. This is not surprising since there is prodigious shrimp and "baitfish" production associated with the Mississippi River plume dynamics and the substantial reef fisheries on coastal shelf areas around the Gulf.   For example, Gulf menhaden currently produces the second largest annual tonnage of fish catches in the entire United States, while Gulf shrimp are number one nationally in economic value. While the Gulf is famous for its extensive red snapper and reef fish fisheries, it is also an important natal ground for sailfish, marlins and tunas.   But that seascape is rapidly changing due to explosive growth of recreational fishing throughout the Gulf of Mexico and its enormous economic impacts.   Currently, recreational tarpon fishing alone is a $5-7 billion annual industry in the Gulf of Mexico. In fact, the world-famous Florida marine recreational fishing industry is now 10 times more valuable than commercial fishing, and now more valuable than the historically dominant Florida citrus industry!

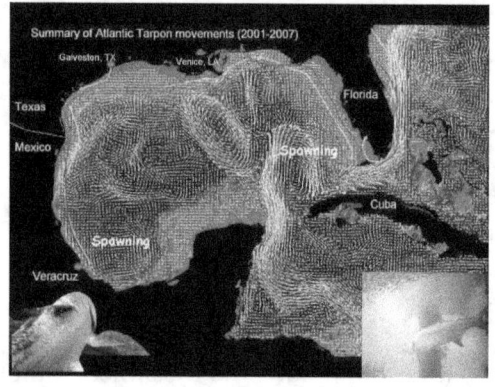

So, management for sustainability of the Gulf's precious fishery resources will take new perspectives. For example, the concept of "connectivity" needs to be considered from a much broader perspective, not only in terms of larval transport – but also that of adults that can actively move relatively great distances around the region.   Recent satellite-based PAT (passive archival transmitting) tagging studies have shown that tarpon move widely throughout the Gulf of Mexico and southeast US region.   Fish appear to spawn off of Mexico, feeding off of Louisiana, and tarpon also spawn off of the West Florida shelf. Seasonally fish move north to US waters from Veracruz, Mexico, and the Gulf of Campeche to off Galveston, Texas, then on to Louisiana and Mississippi from the west; and up along the Florida Keys and west Florida shelf to Alabama, Mississippi and Louisiana from the east. So the real question is "are our tarpon their tarpon?", and what specific management regimes will sustain this multibillion-dollar industry? A sad related story about the unquantified killing fields is reflected in the observation that, in May 2007, a Veracruz, Mexico, fishing tournament killed 73 large tarpon in about 3 fishing days, amounting to 10,243 pounds (or > 5 tons) of large, mature tarpon! These are fish that to live to very old ages (>80 years) and are highly vulnerable to precipitous stock declines with fishing The result is a very substantial impact on the spawning stock of such a old and highly vulnerable fishery resource of substantial economic value to the region   The Gulf of Mexico initiative to sustain the economically- and ecologically-valuable fisheries must recognize all solutions run through Mexico!

In summary, the Gulf of Mexico ecosystem is a highly dynamic coupled biophysical environment. Shelf waters <30 fathoms account for >70% of the fishery landings, and these are highly susceptible to human and natural impacts. The regional ecosystem is under significant anthropogenic & environmental stresses. Management strategies for sustainability of this valuable ecosystem requires development of a systems approach that also protects habitats that support a broad range of fisheries productivity. Ensuring sustainable fisheries and economics will require strategic inter-state and international cooperation and partnerships in both science and management.

Ecological Studies in the Shelf-Edge Reserves Madison Swanson and Steamboat Lumps of the Northeast Gulf of Mexico: A Summary of Research Studies

Christopher Koenig and Felicia Coleman
Florida State University, Coastal and Marine Laboratory, St. Teresa, FL

The experimental marine reserves Madison Swanson (coordinates of corners: NE, N27° 17' W085° 38'; NW, N29° 17' W085° 50'; SE, N29° 06' W085° 38'; SW, N29° 06' W085° 50') and Steamboat Lumps (coordinates of corners: NE, N28° 14' W084° 37'; NW, N28° 14' W084° 48'; SE, N28° 03' W084° 37'; SW, N28° 03' W084° 48') are located on the shelf edge (50 – 120 m deep) of the northeastern Gulf of Mexico, an area of high reef fish fishery production with abundant gag spawning aggregations (Koenig et al. 1996). These reserves were closed to all bottom fishing in June 2000 primarily to allow the study of fishing-induced sex ratio alteration in gag (*Mycteroperca microlepis*). (Gag males were shown by multiple studies (e.g., Coleman et al. 1996, McGovern et al. 1998) to decline from 20 to 25% of the adult population in the 1970s to 2 to 5% in the 1990s both in the Gulf of Mexico and South Atlantic regions of the SE United States.) Important priorities in these reserves, in addition to gag sex ratio studies, were to evaluate the demographics, and the behavioral and reproductive ecology of dominant fishery species, including scamp (*M. phenax*), red grouper (*Epinephelus morio*), and red snapper (*Lutjanus campechanus*). An initial closure period of four years was recommended by the Gulf of Mexico Fishery Management Council, but commercial and recreational fisher support prompted the Council to close the reserves for an additional 6 years. Sunset is now scheduled for 2010.

Our first objectives within the reserves were to map and characterize spawning habitat for gag and the other fishery species. Kathy Scanlon (USGS-Woods Hole; Scanlon et al. 2001) produced sidescan sonar images of both reserves in 2001 and Jim Gardner, then of USGS, produced high-resolution multibeam images in the following years. We used the geo-referenced sidescan images to conduct submersible surveys of the benthic habitat on the Sustainable Seas Expedition aboard the R/V Gordon Gunter. Commercial fishermen showed us the locations of gag spawning sites and red grouper habitat within and outside of the reserves. We mapped these sites and characterized the habitat.

We focused our studies in Madison Swanson because the major gag spawning habitat occurred there; Steamboat Lumps contained primarily red grouper habitat. We selected 15 gag aggregation sites within the reserve and compared these with 15 outside in terms of demographics and movement patterns. Home ranges were evaluated inside through the use of acoustic telemetry tags. Densities within and around Madison Swanson was estimated with an ROV (support from NOAA NURC-Wilmington). The reproductive behavior and excavating behavior of red grouper was studied in Steamboat Lumps aboard the R/V Bellows (FIO support).

To meet our objectives we first had to develop methods to capture the reef fish at shelf-edge depths and bring them to the surface for sampling, tagging, and release. We developed a method of trapping and venting the fish at depths of about 40% of depth of capture (i.e., before any damaging effects of gas expansion could occur), then slowly bringing them to the surface.

Various samples were taken from captured fish including gonads for determination of reproductive state and sex, tissue samples for ongoing genetic studies, and fin rays for age determination. Fish were measured, then tagged and released. Tagging involved both conventional dart tags and acoustic telemetry tags (Vemco).

Results of our three-year study showed low rates of movement by gag and red snapper and extremely low rates of movement by red grouper. The sedentary nature of red grouper is undoubtedly related to their investment of considerable energy in habitat construction (Coleman et al. in preparation). We continued our demographic studies for 3 years using commercial and charter vessels. During this work we observed poaching by commercial and recreational vessels nearly every trip and these vessels were often fishing on our research sites. The primary target of commercial fishermen was gag, as know poachers were observed by several honest fishermen unloading mostly gag at the docks. According to these honest fishermen, the catch rate of the commercial poachers was over 1000 lb per day. Clearly, the accuracy of our data, especially for gag, has been compromised.

The intensity of poaching increased as hurricanes in the Gulf increased in frequency, with hurricane Ivan in 2004 and hurricanes Katrina and Rita in 2005. Coast Guard officials admitted that they had to divert nearly all of their assets to the sites of storm destruction and neglected surveillance and enforcement of the reserves. As a result of this intense poaching we could not show any significant differences in size or age for gag inside relative to outside the reserves, but population densities were significantly higher inside. The percentage of males was significantly higher (at 8% males) inside the reserve than outside only in 2003, but rapidly declined to background levels, as poaching intensity increased. The other three species, scamp, red grouper, and red snapper all showed a significant greater size and age inside relative to outside. These results combined with data showing relatively small home ranges in all these species indicate that the size of these reserves (about 10 x 10 nm each) is sufficiently large to protect the size and age structure of the spawners. Now that commercial vessels are being continuously tracked with VMS (vessel monitoring systems; i.e., satellite tracking) commercial poaching has fallen to near zero. Our present work will evaluate the reserve effect on gag in the absence of poaching.

Telemetry data indicated male gag remained within close proximity of the spawning sites year round. This behavior makes males more vulnerable to fishing after the spawning season when most females have traveled from shelf-edge spawning sites to shelf habitat. This is because males make up a greater proportion of the gag population on the aggregation sites after the spawning season. This information, combined with the timing of sex change, provides the basis for our conceptual model of fishing-induced sex ratio alteration (Koenig et al. in preparation). Historical data on the occurrence of transitionals (individuals in the process of sex change) indicate sex change is initiated during the spawning period (i.e., transitionals appear in the months after spawning). Because fishers fish spawning sites year round (Koenig personal observation) they catch males and transitionals mostly after the spawning period, which is reflected in the historical catch data. Therefore the appropriate management action to protect males is to close an area, not a season.

Large male and female red snapper appear to behave similar to male gag in that they remain around their spawning sites year round. Although our telemetry sample size is small and tagged fish were likely lost to poaching, we found one individual remaining around the same spawning site for over 2 years and two others remaining for about a year. These data suggest that shelf-edge spawning of red snapper could be protected my marine reserves of the size of Madison Swanson. In our ongoing studies we are using acoustic telemetry to further evaluate spawning aggregation formation by red snapper on the shelf edge.

Red grouper spawning behavior was observed and recorded in Steamboat Lumps using an ROV outfitted with a hydrophone. We found that red grouper exhibit a lek-like mating system; females swim into male territories and spawning ensues. During courtship males and females adopt distinctive color patterns and males produce a specific spawning sound just prior to spawning. We are continuing this work on a NOAA NURC-Wilmington-sponsored cruise scheduled for May 2008. Specific spawning sounds open the possibility of locating dominant spawning areas through the use of towed listening arrays. In addition, specific spawning sounds of commercially important species could provide NMFS stock assessment with direct estimates of spawning frequencies in fished relative to the unfished populations within the reserves.

The most interesting behavior we discovered is red grouper excavating behavior. It is interesting because it casts them in the role of keystone species (a species whose ecological position is heavily supportive of other species within that ecosystem). That is, they create reef habitat that is used by many other species. Our experiments (mostly on juveniles in Florida Bay) and observations on the shelf edge show that red grouper expose habitat (or substrate) for many other reef species, including other fishes, motile invertebrates, and sessile invertebrates such as corals and sponges (Coleman et al. in preparation). We found that red grouper begin to dig soon after metamorphosis (Colin et al. 1996) and continue that behavior throughout their lives. Historically, before they were overfished, red grouper were likely responsible for exposing extensive ledge and other rocky habitat after major storms occluded them through siltation. To evaluate the importance of their role as habitat engineers on shelf habitat it would require additional experimental reserves in shallower areas where storms have a significant effect on sediment movements to evaluate their impact on the exposure of reef habitat and the use of that habitat by other species. It is ironic that we spend considerable funds constructing artificial reefs, yet we decimate the very species that exposes and maintains reef habitat.

We are presently evaluating the connectivity of shelf-edge habitat of the NE Gulf of Mexico with adjacent systems, such as the Big Bend seagrass and saltmarsh habitat and the Apalachicola drainage, which contributes nutrient-rich water along the shelf edge known as the "Green River Phenomenon". Trophic subsidies from the Big Bend estuaries arrive in the grouper's territory in the form of small fishes, especially pinfish. Through the use of stable isotopes we are evaluating the contribution of these estuarine species to grouper production and reproduction. Nutrient rich Apalachicola water extending out onto the shelf edge may be contributing to benthic production through benthic—pelagic coupling mechanisms, but the details are unknown at this time. We also suspect that nutrient rich Apalachicola water delivered to the shelf edge during gag spawning may contribute to larval survival. We suspect that these adjacent ecosystems are strongly interdependent and that fishery production relies on external subsidies. That is our working hypothesis.

References

Coleman, F. C. , C.C. Koenig, L. A. Collins. 1996. Reproductive styles of shallow-water grouper species (Pisces: Serranidae) in the eastern Gulf of Mexico and the consequences of fishing spawning aggregations. *Environmental Biology of Fishes* 47, 129-141.

Colin, P.L., C. C. Koenig, & W. Laroche. 1996. Development from egg to juvenile of the red grouper, *Epinephelus morio*, in the laboratory. *In* F. Arreguin-Sanchez, J. L. Munro, M. C. Balgos & D. Pauly (eds.). Biology, fisheries & culture of tropical groupers and snappers. ICLARM Conf. Proc. 48, 449 p.

Koenig, C. C., F. C. Coleman, L. A. Collins, Y. Sadovy, P. L. Colin. 1996. Reproduction in gag, *Mycteroperca microlepis*, in the eastern Gulf of Mexico, pp. 307-323. *In* F. Arreguin-Sanchez, J. L. Munro, M. C. *Balgos & D. Pauly (eds.). Biology, fisheries & culture of tropical groupers and snappers. ICLARM Conf. Proc.* 48, 449 p.

McGovern, J. et al. 1998. Changes in sex ratio and size at maturity of gag, Mycteroperca microlepis, from the Atlantic coast of the southeastern United States during 1976 – 1995. *Fish. Bull.* 96: 797-807.

The Timing and Location of Reef Fish Spawning Aggregations in Belize and the Cayman Islands: Insights for the Design of a Protected Areas Network in the Gulf of Mexico

Will Heyman

Department of Geography, Texas A&M University, College Station, TX

Introduction

This brief paper provides a summary of a talk presented at the Mote Marine Laboratory on 23 January 2008, within a NOAA-sponsored symposium called, *Islands in the Stream*. The concept behind this symposium was to evaluate the existing scientific evidence and support for the possible development of a bi-national system of marine protected areas spanning the Gulf of Mexico that together confer resilience to this valuable system, in the face of localized, regional, and global threats. The *Islands in the Stream* concept is that topographic highs that rise abruptly and significantly above the otherwise relatively flat coastal margin within the Gulf, e.g. shelf edges, sea mounts, salt domes, ridges, and pinnacles are likely important for both fisheries productivity and marine biodiversity conservation and should therefore be seriously considered as core areas within a proposed network of marine reserves within the Gulf of Mexico. While my work has not taken place within the Gulf of Mexico, recent findings from Belize and the Cayman Islands may provide corollary support to the Islands in the stream concept.

Multi-species Reef Fish Spawning Aggregations in Belize

Spawning aggregations serve as source sites for eggs and larvae of most reef fishes and are therefore considered essential life habitat and critical conservation targets. The Belize Spawning Aggregation Working group, a consortium of government and non-government and educational institutions and organizations, evaluated several known or historical Nassau grouper (*Epinephelus striatus*) spawning aggregation sites with similar geomorphology for the presence of Nassau grouper (and other species') spawning aggregations between 2001 and 2004. A standard monitoring protocol and database were used to collect and compile the data form at least 13 sites throughout Belize (Heyman and Adrian, 2006) (Figure 1). These data were collected in part to test the following hypothesis (Heyman, 2004).

Hypothesis: Transient multi-species reef fish spawning aggregations occur at locations with the following characteristics:
- Reef promontory (inflections on the reef)
- Shelf edge
- 25 – 50 m depth
- Adjacent to deep waters (> 500 m)
- Windward facing

Fig. 1

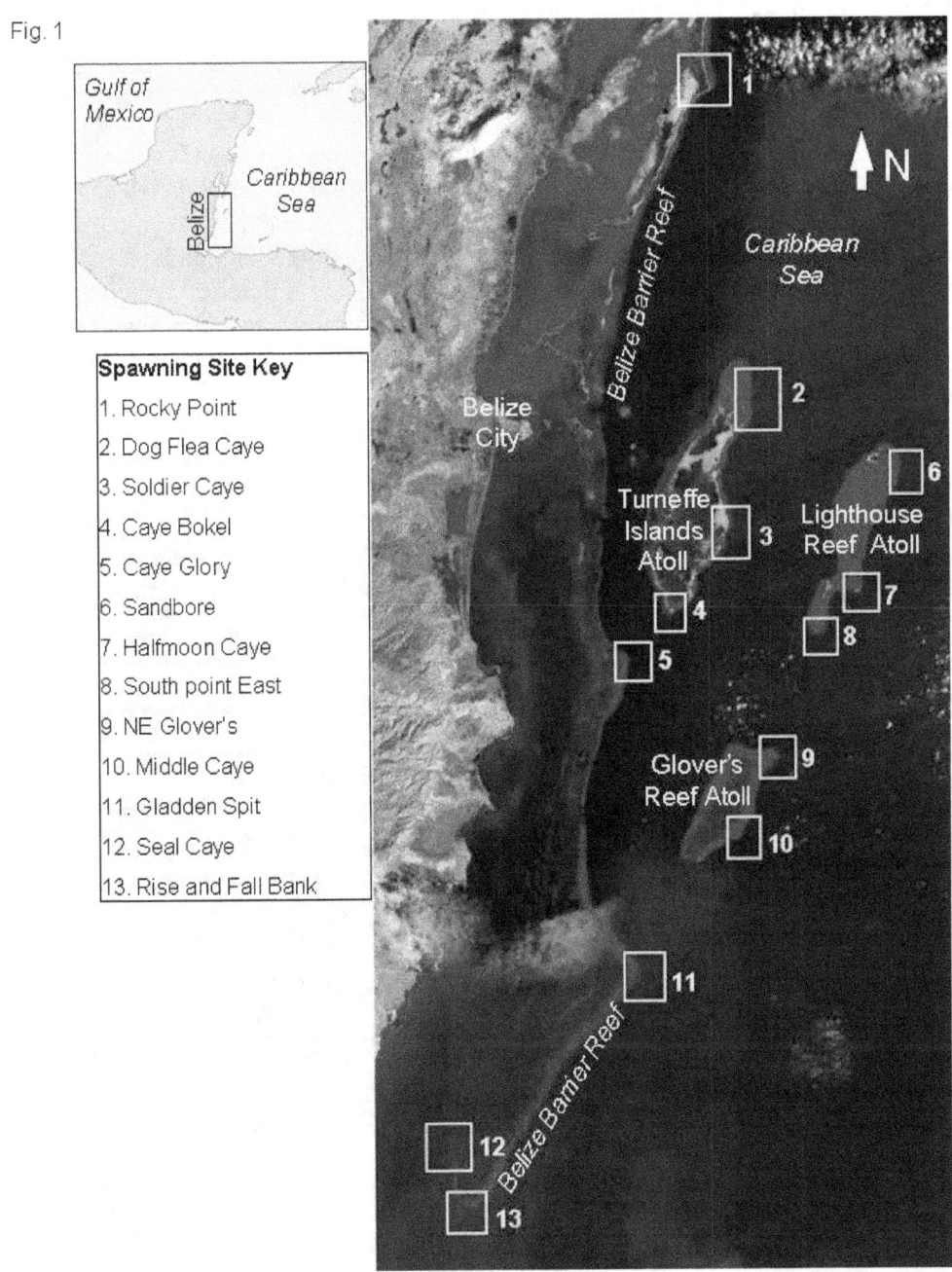

Spawning Site Key
1. Rocky Point
2. Dog Flea Caye
3. Soldier Caye
4. Caye Bokel
5. Caye Glory
6. Sandbore
7. Halfmoon Caye
8. South point East
9. NE Glover's
10. Middle Caye
11. Gladden Spit
12. Seal Caye
13. Rise and Fall Bank

Figure 1. Reef fish spawning aggregation sites in Belize.

The best-studied spawning aggregation site in Belize is Gladden Spit, a reef promontory on the Belize Barrier Reef (Figures 1 and 2). The site provides habitat for transient spawning aggregations for at least 17 species from 6 families throughout all times of year. Aggregating species that have been documented to spawn at the site include some of the most commercially important reef fish in the Caribbean including Nassau grouper (*Epinephelus striatus*), Black grouper (*Mycteroperca bonaci*), Cubera snapper (*Lutjanus cyanopterus*), and Mutton snapper (*Lutjanus analis*) (Heyman et al. 2001; 2005; in press). Each species aggregates with striking site and temporal fidelity within a 6 ha area at the tip of the Gladden Spit reef promontory. The geomorphology of the spawning site was evaluated using a detailed bathymetric map (Figure 1) (Heyman et al., 2007). The spawning aggregations form in 25 – 40 m water depth, at the tip of a windward facing reef promontory, on a shelf edge, adjacent to deep (> 500 m) water. Data collected at Gladden Spit are consistent with and provide support for the conceptual hypothesis presented above.

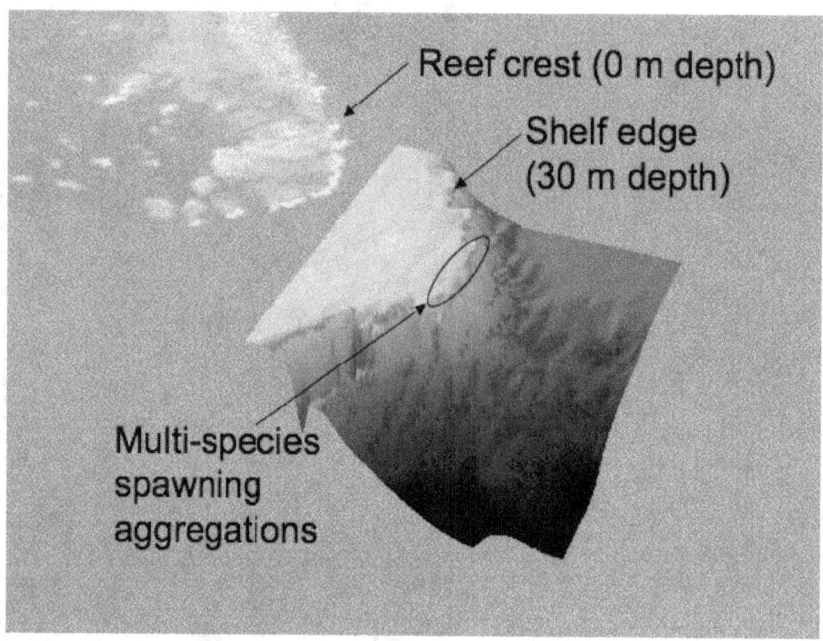

Figure 2: Gladden Spit in Belize illustrating the relationship between the multi-species spawning aggregation sites and the reef crest, shelf break and deep waters. The deepest area is indicated by the darkest color and is approximately 700 m.

Several other sites in Belize have geomorphology that is similar to Gladden Spit, and also harbor multi-species spawning aggregations (numbered sites in Figure 2). Based on data collected by the Belize Spawning Aggregations Working Committee, and with the support of local fishermen, the Minister of Fisheries declared a closed season for Nassau grouper and declared 11 of the sites as new marine reserves (Government of Belize 2003a; 2003b). Data collected at these other sites are largely consistent with and provide additional support to the conceptual hypothesis.

Five historical Nassau grouper spawning aggregation sites have been identified in the Cayman Islands and each of these sites occur near reef promontories, shelf breaks, and adjacent to deep water, though some of these sites are windward, others are leeward. Though full characterizations have not been completed at any of the sites, the Department of Environment indicates that West End, Little Cayman harbors spawning aggregations of various grouper and snapper species throughout the year (P. Bush personal communication) and spawning was documented for several transient spawning species at the site (Whaylen et al., 1994).

Conclusion

In conclusion, there is a growing body of evidence from Belize, the Cayman Islands, and other sites in the Caribbean that at least some portion of transient multi-species reef fish spawning aggregations occur at the shelf break of windward facing reef promontories. Additional examples of spawning aggregations at similar abrupt changes in slope are found in other parts of the Caribbean (e.g. Cuba and Puerto Rico), Florida (e.g. Riley's Hump) and the Gulf of Mexico (Koenig et al., 2000; Koenig, this symposium). The location of multi-species reef fish spawning aggregations may be similarly focused around the Islands in the Stream of the Gulf of Mexico.

References

Government of Belize (2003a) Statutory instrument no. 161 of 2003. Fisheries (spawning aggregation site reserves) order, 2003. 161:1-8

Government of Belize (2003b). Statutory instrument no. 162 of 2003. Fisheries (Nassau grouper protection) regulations, 2003. 162:1-2

Heyman, W.D. 2004. Conservation of multi-species spawning aggregation sites. *Proceedings of the Gulf and Caribbean Fisheries Institute.* 55:521-529.

Heyman, W.D. and G. Adrien. 2006. A protocol and database for monitoring transient multi-species reef fish spawning aggregations in the Mesoamerican reef. *Proceedings of the Gulf and Caribbean Fisheries Institute.* 57:445-462.

Heyman, W.D., J-L.B. Ecochard, and F.B. Biasi. 2007. Low-cost bathymetric mapping for tropical marine conservation – a focus on reef fish spawning aggregation sites. *Marine Geodesy.* 30(1): 37-50.

Heyman, Ezer, T., D.V. Thattai, B. Kjerfve and W.D. Heyman. 2005. On the variability of the flow along the Meso-American Barrier Reef System: A numerical model study of the influence of the Caribbean Current and eddies. *Ocean Dynamics.* 55:458-475.

Heyman, W.D., B. Kjerfve, and T. Ezer. Mesoamerican Reef spawning aggregations help maintain fish populations: a review of connectivity research and priorities for science and management. *NOAA Marine Conservation Science Series.* In press.

Heyman, W.D., B. Kjerfve, R.E. Johannes, R. Graham. 2001. Whale sharks, *Rhincodon typus*, aggregate to feed on fish spawn in Belize. *Marine Ecology Progress Series.* 215: 275-282.

Heyman, W.D., B. Kjerfve, K.L. Rhodes, R.T. Graham, and L. Garbutt. 2005. Cubera snapper, *Lutjanus cyanopterus*, spawning aggregations on the Belize Barrier Reef over a six year period. *Journal of Fish Biology* 67(1):83-101.

Koenig, C. C., F. C. Coleman, C. B. Grimes, G. R. Fitzhugh, K. M. Scanlon, C. T. Gledhill, and M. Grace. 2000. Protection of fish spawning habitat for the conservation of warm-temperate reef-fish fisheries of shelf-edge reefs of Florida. Bulletin of Marine Science. 66(3):593-616.

Whaylen L., C.V. Pattengill-Semmens, B.X. Semmens, P.G. Bush, M.R. Boardman. 2004. Observations of a Nassau grouper, *Epinephelus striatus*, spawning aggregation site in Little Cayman, Cayman Islands, including multi-species spawning information. Environmental Biology of Fishes 70(3):305-313.

Panel 4 Discussion

Jerry Ault (University of Miami/RSMAS) – presentation/panelist
Chris Koenig (Florida State University) – presentation/panelist
Will Heyman (Texas A&M University) – presentation/panelist
Jim Bohnsack (NOAA National Marine Fishery Service) - panelist
Doug Weaver (Texas A&M University) – panelist

(from meeting transcripts)

Jim Hendee: Have you noted specific physical cues besides lunar periodicity that influences them to spawn?

Chris Koening: Spawning site selection appears to be dominated by shelf edge precipices or breaks. If there are rocks along those breaks they'll be there. These are consistent sites. They are consistent over long periods of time. Madison Swanson was pretty much fished out when it became a reserve. The fish reestablished within a short period of time. With regard to the spawning timing, we don't know. Gag grouper appear to spawn late in the afternoon.

Jerry Ault: Black grouper are known to spawn in West Florida Shelf like clockwork. Tarpon periodicity was 3-4 days prior to the new and full moon. Diving to 150 meters. Lunar and thermal events help cycle it. Go back to relatively the same area as it facilitates survivorship.

Will Heyman: Seeing fidelity to sites – geomorphologic cues, as well as seasonal and lunar and diel cues. We've looked at the currents in some of these locations. Thinking some of the currents may be different at these promontories. Currents faster and more variable than in other areas.

Andy Shepard: Valuable fisheries are coastal. How important will these areas that are offshore be to these coastal fish?

Jerry Ault: May be complementary to some of the areas we need to protect to capture important areas of the life history. Important to protect representative habitats for different aspects of the life history.

Lori Arguelles: For the proposed sites under consideration for this effort – is it adequate? Is it less than what is needed? Can you give context for this?

Jerry Ault: Jim Bohnsack proposed about 20% of available habitat ought to be protected. That was just a guess. It's not clear – comes down to winnowing down the objectives. It's a good start.

Chris Koenig: Requires an understanding of the species life history. We have a number of spawning aggregations being protected, but no one is protecting the pre spawning population. They are completely unprotected and they are getting hammered.

Jerry Ault: Won't sustain the productivity because they won't protect the smaller animals that are getting targeted as they cross the shelf. We need to attend to the cross shelf issues.

Doug Weaver: the list of candidate sites is very inclusive and covers most of the spectacular sites in the Gulf. We are comprehensive in scope – it's just a matter of what "MPA" means – it's not all going to be no-take. Not just large predators – we've focused on some of the large predators, etc. These other categories of species are important, too. There are connections with the planktivores and the top predators, too.

(Speaker Not Identified, addressed to the Panel): Why hasn't the Elbow, just south of the Florida Middle Grounds, been included in this concept?

Kim Ritchie: We will have time to cover this type of information as a group in the final discussions.

Dan Basta: We are changing the landscape of how you look at your data. We're looking for those special places where the you get the most bang for your buck. In order to do that you have to do this one species at a time (understand the life history). Takes a lot of time. We don't have time to do all of that to bring an idea forward with the "Islands in the Stream". So where do you start and where does it have to go? These kinds of networks can be established with guidance regarding where we need to go.

Jerry Ault: There are data that exist that can help us to begin to paint out where those should be. There needs to be a feedback mechanism to help refine those data. This is an iterative process that closes in on reality.

Al Hine: Are fish using seafloor cues to find spawning sites?

Will Heyman: I have a student starting to look at that.

Walt Jaap: fish use electromagnetic cues, too.

Panel 5: Existing Legal Structure/ Regulations in the Gulf of Mexico

Moderator: Brian Keller

HAPC and Other Habitat or Area Based Regulations
(January 17, 2008)

Shepherd Grimes
NOAA General Council, NMFS, St. Petersburg FL

Habitat areas of particular concern (HAPC), is a concept created in the regulatory guidelines required pursuant to the essential fish habitat (EFH) provisions of the Manuson-Stevens Act. The concept is intended to encourage fishery management councils to create subsets of EFH, which are comprised of habitat areas that generally have some exceptional characteristics. While the HAPC designation itself carries no additional legal protection, conceptually the designation indicates a need for some additional consideration. In the Gulf, additional protection afforded to HAPC is variable, and based on a case-by-case determination by the fishery management councils and NMFS. HAPC is only one example of potential area based protective measures that may be implemented under the Magnuson-Stevens Act (MSA). There are numerous such measures in the current federal regulations applicable to the Gulf exclusive economic zone (EEZ), and they have been implemented to achieve a variety of objectives, many of which do not relate specifically to habitat protection. In addition, there are other federal statutes, including the National Marine Sanctuaries Act, which may be used either in conjunction with the MSA, or separate from the MSA to create area based restrictions.

The regulatory provisions specific to HAPC designation, as well as other area based fishing restrictions in the Gulf of Mexico, are available in Appendix A.

Minerals Management Service:
Protection of Sensitive Habitats on the Outer Continental Shelf of the Gulf of Mexico

James E. Sinclair
Minerals Management Service, Metairie, LA

The U.S. Department of the Interior's Minerals Management Service (MMS) has protected sensitive offshore habitats from potential impacts by oil and gas activities on the Outer Continental Shelf (OCS) since the early 1970's. Decades of research and monitoring provide the scientific basis for protection of these biologically important ecosystems. Current regulations include lease stipulations, with specific details in official Notices to Lessees and Operators (NTL's) and other documents (http://www.gomr.mms.gov/homepg/regulate/regs/ntlltl.html). Much of the current MMS environmental regulations are described in NTL's 2004-G05 (Biologically Sensitive Areas), 2000-G20 (Chemosynthetic Communities), and 2003-G03 (Remotely Operated Vehicle Surveys). This document is a brief summary of the regulations designed to protect sensitive habitats in U.S. Federal waters of the Gulf of Mexico (GOM). For a full description, refer to the appropriate regulatory documents.

There are four general categories of sensitive habitats protected by MMS in the Gulf of Mexico: live bottoms, topographic features, potentially sensitive biological features (PSBF's), and chemosynthetic communities.

LIVE BOTTOMS include two subcategories: low-relief and the Pinnacle Trend. Low-relief live bottoms include seagrass meadows and hard-bottom areas of about 1-2 m (3-6 ft) or less relief in the Eastern GOM. Small hard-bottom features support various invertebrate fauna and fish communities. Many areas of the west Florida shelf are composed of flat limestone substrate with a veneer of sand. These areas support ephemeral algae communities that come and go as the sand shifts locations. Many of these areas support invertebrates that persist by growing tall enough to stand above the shifting sand.

The Pinnacle Trend is an area of widely scattered features ranging from low-relief rocky areas to major pinnacles, as well as ridges, scarps, relict patch reefs, fields of low mounds, and fields of shallow depressions. Seventy MMS lease blocks (3 mi x 3 mi square) carry the Live Bottom (Pinnacle Trend) Stipulation. This area is about 65 km (40 mi) east of the mouth of the Mississippi River.

No bottom-disturbing activities may cause direct impacts to live-bottoms features. Proposed activities in blocks with the Live Bottom (Pinnacle Trend) Stipulation require a live-bottom survey report that contains detailed bathymetry of the area out to 1,000 m (3,280 ft) beyond the proposed activity. If activities are near live bottoms, the operator must submit a map with 2-ft contour intervals, the delineation of live bottoms, the height of seafloor features, the location of proposed wells, and the location of anchors, cables, chains, etc. Operators may be required to use a remotely operated vehicle for the clearance of anchor or pipeline positions. The MMS will require measures to protect live-bottom areas including, but not limited to, the following: (a) relocation of operations; (b) shunting of all drilling fluids and cuttings; (c) transportation of drilling fluids and cuttings to approved disposal sites; and (d) monitoring of live bottoms. After the activity, operators must submit a map showing the locations of bottom disturbances.

TOPOGRAPHIC FEATURES are hard banks in the GOM formed by the uplift of rocks by salt diapirs. These habitats are elevated above surrounding soft bottoms into less turbid mid-waters with greater penetration of sunlight. As a result, reef communities develop that include many of the more sensitive species associated with Caribbean waters.

Lease stipulations establish five categories of protection zones. The MMS protects 37 banks in the Central and Western GOM. The Biological Stipulation Map Package includes drawings of each bank with its associated zones. The five protection zones are the No Activity Zone, 1,000-Meter Zone, 1-Mile Zone, 3-Mile Zone, and the 4-Mile Zone. Regulations for each of these banks include the No Activity Zone and up to two of the other zones. The No Activity Zone follows the largest closed depth contour of the seafloor around a bank. The others are boundaries around the No Activity Zone that protect a minimum of the stated measure beyond the bank: 1,000 meters or 1, 3, or 4 miles (Figure 1).

The No Activity Zone is an area prohibiting the placement of structures, drilling rigs, pipelines, anchors, anchor chains, wire ropes, or any other bottom disturbance on a bank within the listed isobath, which is generally the largest closed contour line. NTL 2004-G05 further specifies that no such activity shall occur within 500 ft (152 m) of the No Activity Zone.

The 1,000-Meter Zone requires shunting all drill cuttings and drilling fluids to the bottom through a downpipe that terminates an appropriate distance, but no more than 10 m (33 ft), from the bottom. Claypile Bank has the 1,000-Meter Zone but requires monitoring instead of shunting.

The 1-Mile Zone requires shunting all drill cuttings and drilling fluids to the bottom through a downpipe that terminates an appropriate distance, but no more than 10 m (33 ft), from the bottom.

The 3-Mile Zone requires shunting all drill cuttings and drilling fluids from development operations to the bottom through a downpipe that terminates an appropriate distance, but no more than 10 m (33 ft), from the bottom. If more than two exploration wells are to be drilled from the same surface location, drill cuttings and drilling fluids from the exploration drilling operations are to be shunted.

The 4-Mile Zone is in effect only at the East and West Flower Garden Banks. Its requirements are the same as the 1-Mile Zone.

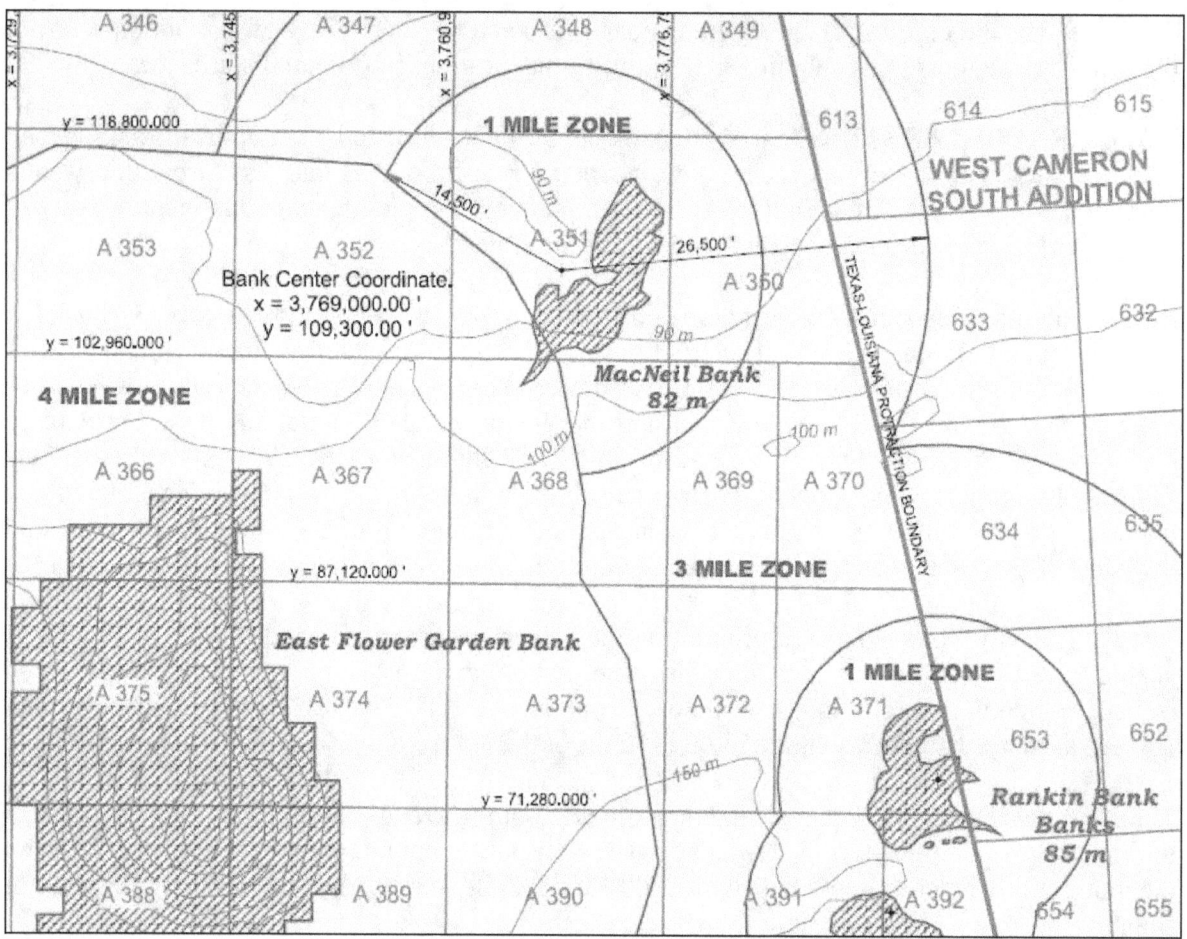

Figure 1. Protection zones stipulated by the MMS on offshore leases near topographic features include the No Activity Zone, 1000-Meter Zone, 1-Mile Zone, 3-Mile Zone, and the 4-Mile Zone. No Activity Zones (red shading) are based on a particular isobath (listed) rather than a map polygon. The No Activity Zone at the Flower Garden Banks is defined by the ¼ ¼ ¼ line that encompasses the 100-m (328-ft) isobath. The 1000-Meter, 1-Mile, and 3-Mile Zones are defined by a radius from a biological centerpoint, as for MacNeil Bank above. The 4-Mile Zone is a specified buffer of at least four miles around the Flower Garden Banks.

POTENTIALLY SENSITIVE BIOLOGICAL FEATURES (PSBF's) are features not protected by a biological lease stipulation that are of moderate to high relief (about 8 ft (2.4 m) or higher), provide surface area for the growth of sessile invertebrates, and attract large numbers of fish. No bottom-disturbing activities may cause direct impacts to potentially sensitive biological features. If activities are near PSBF's, the operator must submit a map with 2-ft contour intervals, the delineation of PSBF's, the height of seafloor features, the location of proposed wells, and the location of anchors, cables, chains, etc. After the activity, they must submit a map showing the locations of bottom disturbances. Figure 2 shows numerous small features outside the No Activity Zone of Bright Bank that would qualify as PSBF's.

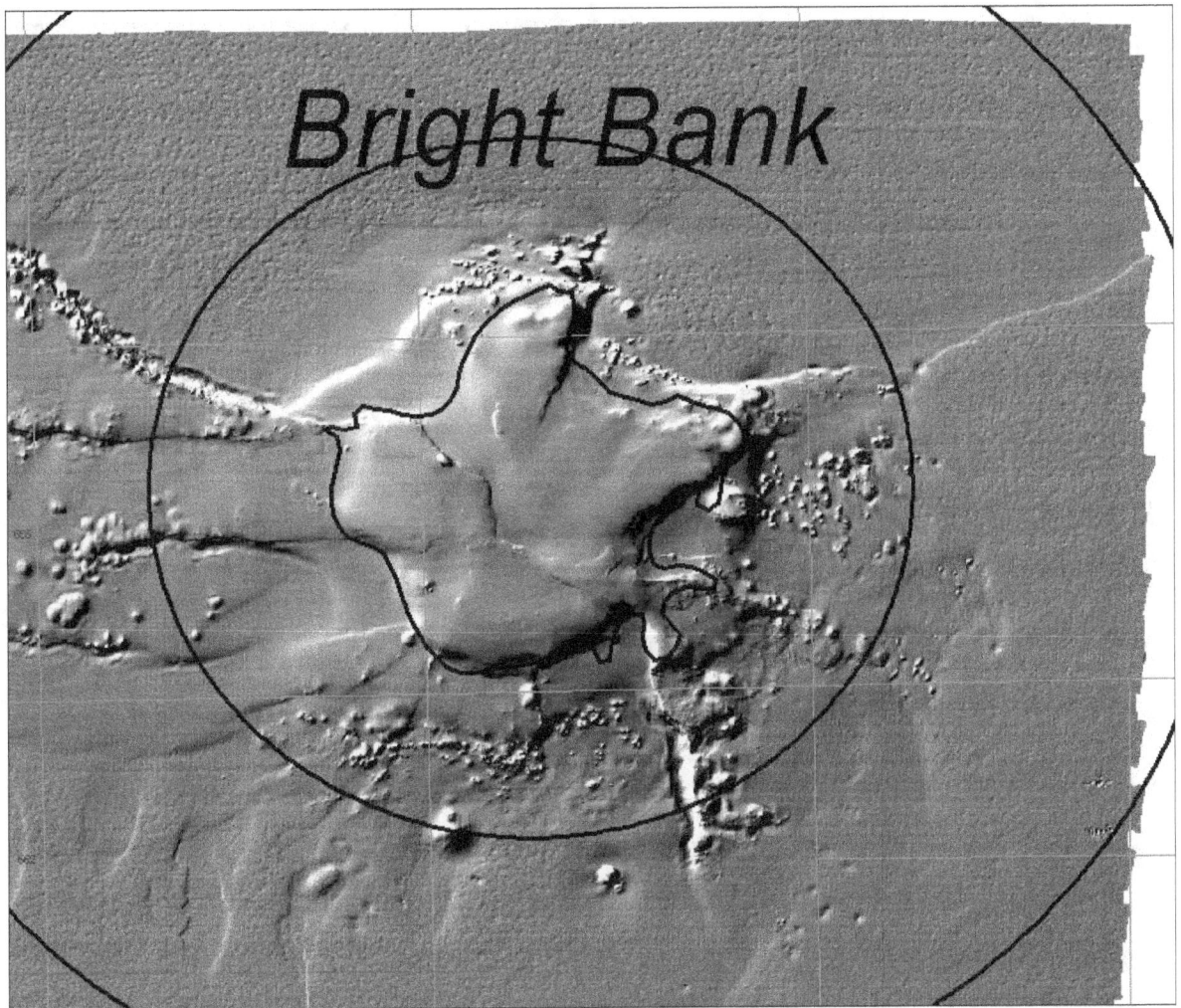

Figure 2. High-resolution multibeam bathymetry reveals numerous small features outside the No Activity Zone of Bright Bank (Gardner et al., 2002). These features would qualify for protection by MMS as potentially sensitive biological features. Oil and gas activities are prohibited from causing physical impacts to these features.

CHEMOSYNTHETIC COMMUNITIES occur in water depths over 400 m (1,312 ft) at seeps of oil, methane, and sulfide. Chemotrophic bacteria colonize these sites, producing food and precipitating carbonate substrate that supports colonies of mussels, clams, and giant tubeworms. These keystone species create the structure that harbors a significant community of other organisms such as crabs, shrimp, anemones, echinoderms, and a variety of fish species. The MMS protects these communities with regulations that restrict wells, cuttings, and drilling fluids to at least 450 m (1,476 ft) away. No bottom disturbances are allowed within 75 m (246 ft). If areas that could support high-density chemosynthetic communities are present, MMS could require the operator to relocate the proposed activities, provide additional information about the seafloor (video surveys), use a remotely operated vehicle to place anchors precisely, monitor impacts, or any other condition deemed necessary to protect the environment.

These rules also protect other deep hard-bottom communities. In some locations, stony corals colonize the hard-bottom substrate created by chemosynthetic communities, forming deep coral reef communities. *Lophelia pertusa* and *Madrepora oculata* can form dense thickets on the periphery of chemosynthetic communities or on defunct sites that no longer have active seeps. The conditions observed with remote-sensing techniques appear the same for both chemosynthetic communities and deep coral communities. Therefore, the regulations for chemosynthetic communities also protect corals.

Reference

Gardner, J.V., J.D. Beaudoin, J.E.H. Clarke, and P. Dartnell. 2002. Multibeam mapping of selected areas of the Outer Continental Shelf, northwestern Gulf of Mexico — Data, images, and GIS. U.S. Dept. of the Interior, Geological Survey. Open-File Report 02-411. Internet website: http://geopubs.wr.usgs.gov/open-file/of02-411/index.html.

Panel 5 Discussion

Shepherd Grimes (NOAA General Council) – presentation/panelist
Jim Sinclair (Minerals Management Service) – presentation/panelist

(from meeting transcripts)

Barbara Lausche: Does the gulf have any special designation under IMO? (for James Sinclair): my impression is that you have a massive job with all these areas you are trying to deal with. What capacity do you have for monitoring? How are you able to monitor? Have you had to deal with many enforcement actions?

James Sinclair: Yes it is a big job. We have some capacity for monitoring. We have recently acquired a small remotely operated underwater vehicle (ROV) to inspect some of these areas that are below diving depths. We plan to do more of that. As far as enforcement: that's outside my bailiwick. We have a large group (1/3 of MMS field operations folks) that is there function. They have routine inspections and surprise inspections. They have regular oil spill response exercises.

Shepherd Grimes: I don't know regarding IMO question. I don't think there is an agreement between us and Mexico.

John Ogden: One of the strong arguments for "Islands in the Stream" would be to bring the regulations into some harmony. It's mind boggling how effective it could be – strong argument for uniform administration.

Shepherd Grimes: You don't have statutory authority to do that at this point. If you were going to do this under Magnuson you could do this in terms of fisheries.

John Ogden: The end result could be something more cohesive.

James Sinclair: There are activities out there that no body regulates. That's the whole idea here is to establish a system that can protect the habitats from all comers.

Frank Alcock: Shepherd – the report you refer to raised some interesting questions regarding jurisdiction – specifically the Antiquities Act. No precedent regarding the application of the Antiquities Act to areas that don't come above the sea surface.

Shepherd Grimes: The Antiquities Act hadn't until recent times been used as it is now. Wasn't designed to do something as comprehensive as the National Marine Sanctuaries Act for example.

Frank Alcock: There has been a gradual expansion of the use of the act that has been endorsed by Congress and that the Supreme Court have backed up.

Shepherd Grimes: No court as far as I know has decided that yes, this is something that can be done under the Antiquities Act. The Department of Justice has recently opined that it can be done and the Administration has done it.

Frank Alcock: Do you think there will be (lawsuits)?

Shepherd Grimes: My impression is yes.

Tony Grogan: What advantage is there of having the NMS program do this?

Shepherd Grimes: (not captured)

Peg Brady: Can you talk about the range of activities MMS regulates?

James Sinclair: MMS has a lease sale. Before that sale, the industry decides what they want to bid on. There will be stipulations on that lease. They make plans on how they will operate on that lease. They have to submit proposals to MMS which we review thoroughly. They create a plan for developing it, and that goes thru another review. They run pipeline and that process is elaborate – sometimes they share resources. There are routine activities for support activities.

Peg Brady: You are looking at a complete spectrum of activities?

James Sinclair: Yes.

Peg Brady: Are they seeing any of the data that are available to you in terms of biological features?

James Sinclair: The data they have comes mostly from them.

Billy Causey: The idea of having this panel – a lot of people are asking what would this initiative give us that we don't already have? Shepard hit on it early – the Magnuson Stevens Act gives us certain authority, whereas the National Marine Sanctuaries Act has different authorities. Together we're a lot better equipped to accomplish a greater level of conservation.

Ian MacDonald: Incredible infrastructure that the industry provides offshore. All of these structures are potential data gathering nodes. Is there any regulation or legislation that would encourage or require data gathering from these?

James Sinclair: There is some of that – about a year, year and a half ago. MMS requires oil companies to use Acoustic Doppler Current Profiler (ADCPs) on their structures to gather data. There is some of that at least.

Panel 6: Connections with Mexico and the Mesoamerican Barrier Reef System

Moderator: Kim Ritchie

Connectivity of the South Florida Coral Reef Ecosystem to Upstream Waters of the Western Caribbean and Gulf of Mexico

Elizabeth Johns[1] and John Lamkin[2]
[1]Atlantic Oceanographic and Meteorological Laboratory
National Oceanic and Atmospheric Administration, Miami, FL

[2]Southeast Fisheries Science Center,
National Oceanic and Atmospheric Administration, Miami, FL

The coastal waters of southeast Florida, including the coral reefs of NOAA's Florida Keys National Marine Sanctuary (FKNMS), are directly connected by means of strong ocean currents with upstream waters of the western Caribbean Sea and the Gulf of Mexico. In particular, the Caribbean Current and the Loop Current provide a rapid conduit for transport from the Mexican and Belizean coral reefs, located on the eastern shore of the Yucatan Peninsula, into the coastal zone bordered by northern Cuba, south Florida, and Bahamian coral reef ecosystems.

Interdisciplinary cruise data collected in August 2002, March 2006 and January 2007 aboard the NOAA Ship Gordon Gunter, in combination with satellite-tracked surface drifter trajectories and remote sensing imagery, clearly show the highly variable and dynamic nature of the regional current structures, and provide a means of quantifying the potential pathways and rates of transit of the coastal waters and their biological and chemical constituents from one region to another.

Figure 1 shows the trajectories of surface drifters deployed during the March 2006 interdisciplinary cruise along the Mexican Yucatan coastline at 18 to 20 N. Two of the drifters

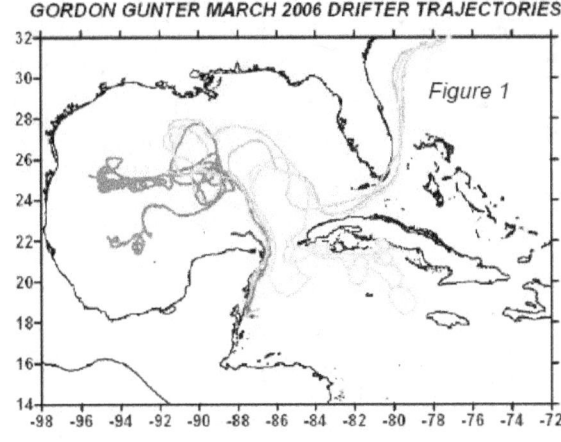

GORDON GUNTER MARCH 2006 DRIFTER TRAJECTORIES

Figure 1

(shown in red and green) became entrained in eddies in the western Gulf of Mexico, one drifter (shown in orange) took a fairly straightforward trip around the Loop Current, through the Straits of Florida and off to the North Atlantic in the Gulf Stream, and one drifter (shown in turquoise) spent several months meandering around the reef areas of southern Cuba before finally rejoining the Loop Current and rapidly exiting out of the area. These drifter trajectories show dramatically the modes of physical connectivity between the coral reef areas of the region.

Figure 2 shows results from another set of surface drifters deployed during the January 2007 cruise. A large cyclonic eddy was discovered in the southern part of the study area offshore of Belize (shown in blue). The rest of the drifters show somewhat simpler paths than last time, all taking the Loop Current pathway into the Florida Straits. One of these drifters (shown in green)

GORDON GUNTER JANUARY 2007 DRIFTER TRAJECTORIES

Figure 2

made a number of transits around the Tortugas Gyre, south of the lower Florida Keys. The drifters also showed a very interesting pattern of lateral dispersion within the Florida Current/Gulf Stream system: The drifter farthest inshore (shown in green) grounded north of Key Largo near the Ocean Reef Club, and the one in the middle (shown in red) grounded to the north near Fort Pierce, while the one closest to the Bahamas (shown in turquoise) actually made a right turn and grounded off Andros Island, thus demonstrating direct connectivity with the Bahamian reefs as well.

Finally, additional drifter trajectories were obtained from the Global Ocean Observing System (GOOS) center, which is based at AOML. The database was searched for all drifters that passed through the box shown in Figure 3 in blue, and the time that it took each drifter to transit from the top of the box at 22 N, to the longitude of the Dry Tortugas at 83 W, was calculated. Quantifying the timing of such transits is important, because larval fish and other creatures have a finite amount of time to travel with the ocean currents before their settlement phase, and the distance and direction that they travel may be critical to their long-term survival.

Figures 3a-3d show examples from this analysis. The drifter shown in Figure 3a, for example, took over three months to make the trip. The drifter shown in Figure 3b took 20 days, and the drifter shown in Figure 3c took only 6 days. The drifter shown in Figure 3d made the fastest transit through the area, traveling from 22 N to the Dry Tortugas in exactly 3 days, at an average speed of 185 cm/s or 3.2 kts.

Results from these cruises, along with ancillary data, show that the study areas are definitely connected to each other with fairly rapid time scales of transport, and furthermore that eddies and gyres play an important role in establishing the relevant time and length scales of connectivity. Such direct physical connectivity by means of strong ocean currents between the coral reef biota of the geographically separated spawning grounds may have an important influence on the degree of biological connectivity between regional larval populations.

Figure 3

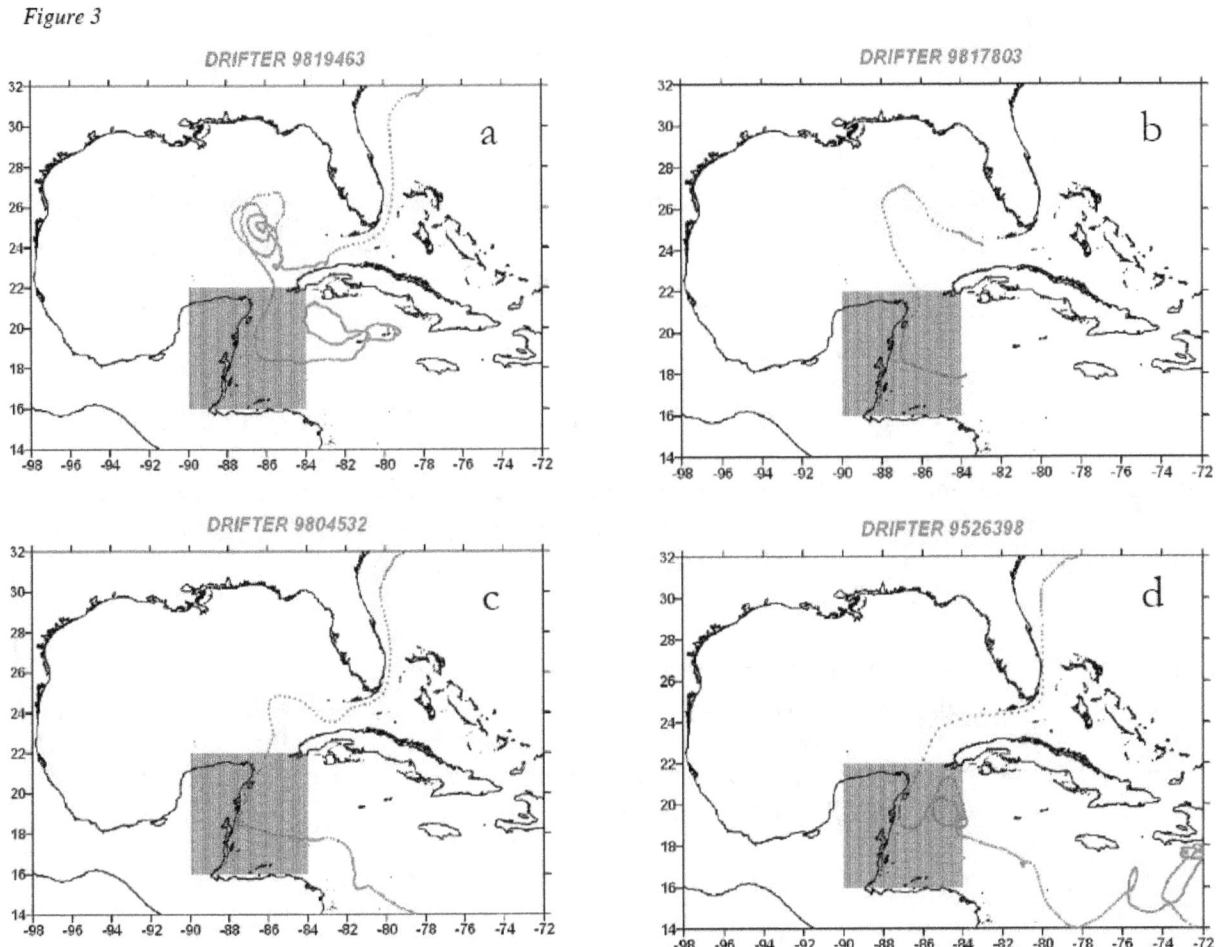

The Mexican Component of the Islands in the Stream Concept

John W. Tunnell, Jr.

Harte Research Institute for Gulf of Mexico Studies, Texas A&M University, Corpus Christi, TX

The Gulf of Mexico should be considered as a natural Large Marine Ecosystem, not influenced by political boundaries. Therefore, to be fully effective, the Islands in the Stream, Gulf of Mexico Marine Protected Areas (MPA) Network should include upstream sites in the southern Gulf of Mexico and Caribbean Sea. Mexico is the nearest and most likely partner in an international component of the extended network. Beyond Mexico to the south, the network could also include the Mesoamerican Barrier Reef System countries of south of Mexico into Belize, Guatemala, and Honduras.

There are 46 named coral reefs in the southern Gulf of Mexico, 31 in the southwestern Gulf off the state of Veracruz, and 15 on the Campeche Bank to the west and north of the Yucatan Peninsula. The majority of the southern Gulf reefs are emergent platform-type coral reefs. In the Mexican Caribbean the Mesoamerican Barrier Reef System starts just south of Cancun and runs as an almost continuous fringing-barrier reef along the entire state of the Quintana Roo, the eastern side of the Yucatan Peninsula.

Preliminary discussions with Dr. Ernesto Enkerlin, Director, and other personnel, of the Comisión Nacional de Áreas Naturales Protegidas (CONANP, National Commission of Natural Protected Areas) within the Secretaría de Medio Ambiente y Recursos Naturales (SEMARNAT, Secretariat of Environmental and Natural Resources) focused on five potential sites in the Mexican component of the MPA network (Figure 1):

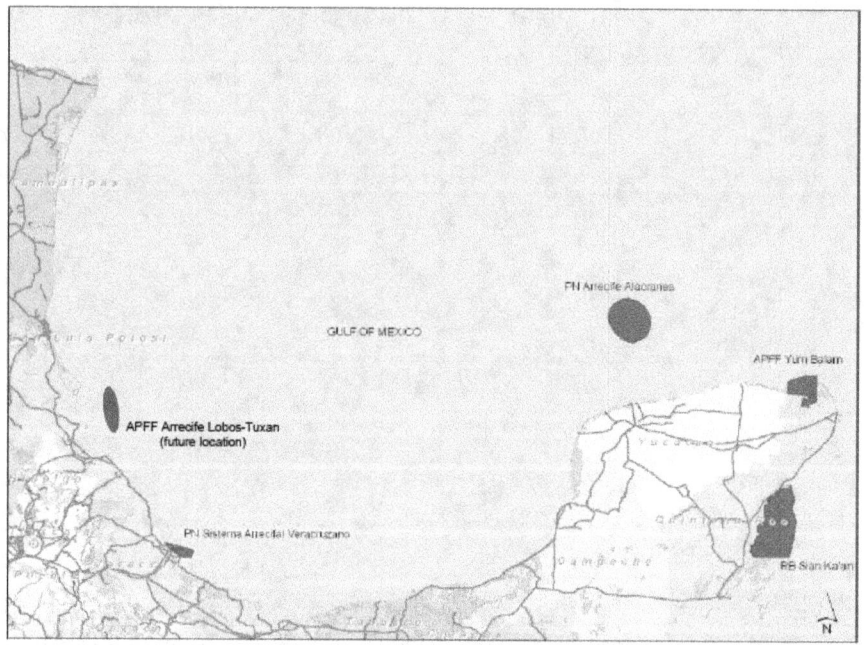

Figure1. – Potential Mexican sites of the Gulf of Mexico Islands in the Stream MPA Network. Blue marks potential sites (see text for details).

Gulf of Mexico Sites –

1.   Lobos – Tuxpan Reefs (Área de Protección de Flora y Fauna [APFF] Arrecifes Lobos-Tuxpan) – six emergent platform coral reefs in northern Veracruz state, currently rated as protected areas for fauna and flora only, but in declaration process for MPA status, perhaps by April 2008.

2.   Veracruz Reef System National Park (Parque Nacional [PN] Sistema Arrecifal Veracruzano) – existing MPA/National Park off the city of Veracruz and fishing village of Anton Lizardo in southern Veracruz state; includes 25 coral reefs total, including 3 fringing, 19 emergent platform reefs, and 3 submerged reef banks.

3.   Alcaran Reef NP (PN Arrecife Alacranes) – existing MPA/National Pak 90 km north of Progresso, Yucatan, northwestern Yucatan Peninsula; very large, atoll-like, emergent platform reef with five islands with extensive seabird colonies and nesting sea turtles.

4.   Yum Balam (APFF Yum Balam) – existing MPA that will be expanded to include the whale shark area and reclassified as the Biosphere Reserve Yum Balam (Reserva de la Biosfera Yum Balam in 2008); located at far northeastern corner of Yucatan Peninsula in the northernmost part of the state of Quintana Roo.

Caribbean Sea Site –

1.   Sian Ka´an Biosphere Reserve (Reserva de la Biosfera Sian Ka´an) – existing MPA/Biosphere Reserve with three planned no-take marine reserves within the northern, central, and southern portion of the Biosphere Reserve; the current Biosphere Reserve includes the fringing-barrier coral reef system, as well as extensive seagrass beds, mangroves, two bays, and upland areas.

Southern Gulf of Mexico coral reefs are typical Caribbean reefs (Tunnell et al. 2007); however, they do have slightly reduced, and decreasing, numbers of purely tropical species as you move further away geographically from the Caribbean. Unlike northern Gulf sites proposed in the Islands in the Stream MPA network, southern Gulf reef sites include emergent reefs and many coral cays or islands. Some of the islands include significant seabird rookeries and sea turtle nesting sites (Figure 2).

Figure 2. – Colonial seabird rookeries on Campeche Bank reef islands: A. Sooty Tern, Isla Perez, Alacran Reef; B. Masked Boobies, Cayo Arenas; C. Red-footed Booby, Isla Desertora, Alacran Reef; D. Brown Noddy, Isla Perez, Alacran Reef; E-F. Magnificent Frigate Birds, Isla Desertora, Alacran Reef, and Cayo Centro, Cayos Arcas, respectively.

Figure 3. – Number of species associated with taxa from southern Gulf of Mexico coral reefs: algae, 305 species; sponges, 28 species; coral, 46 species; gorgonians, 38 species; polychaetes, 41 species; crustaceans, 238 species, mollusks, 555 species; echinoderms, 49 species; and fish, 369 species.

Marine biodiversity on reefs of the southern Gulf of Mexico has been inventoried at over 2000 species (Figure 3), and island biota consists of almost 300 species (Tunnell et al. 2007).

Southern Gulf of Mexico coral reef threats include typical Caribbean-wide threats, such as bleaching, disease, *Diadema* die-off, development, etc.; however, areas closest to population centers and heavy run-off have suffered the most (Table 1).

Table 1. – Status of southern Gulf of Mexico coral reefs by location and major influences.

	Veracruz (SW)		Campeche Bank
	South	**North**	**(SE)**
Rain/Runoff	high	moderate	low
Location	nearshore	mid-shelf	offshore
Population	high	low	low
Condition	Poor	Okay	Good

Working cooperatively and collaboratively with Mexico on the proposed Islands in the Stream MPA Network is imperative for long-term success and connectivity. The upstream reefs serve as sources of larval distribution for U.S. network sites, and they serve as reservoirs for restoration should impacts disturb or affect U.S. sites

Reference

Tunnell, J. W., Jr., E. A. Chavez, and K. Withers. (2007). *Coral Reefs of the Southern Gulf of Mexico*. Texas A&M University Press. College Station, Texas. 256 pp.

The Ocean Tracking Network and the Gulf of Mexico

Robert E. Hueter
Director, Center for Shark Research, Mote Marine Laboratory, Sarasota, FL

The Ocean Tracking Network (OTN, http://www.oceantrackingnetwork.org) is a global initiative designed to comprehensively monitor ocean conditions, and marine life response to those conditions, by using "curtains" of underwater sensors and acoustic receivers deployed at one-kilometer intervals along the sea floor in key areas of the world's oceans (Figs. 1 and 2). The sensors measure oceanographic conditions (conductivity, temperature, depth, current) and the receivers collect acoustic information from transmitters attached to a diversity of marine animals including: migratory fishes such as sharks, tunas and billfishes; sea turtles; marine mammals; and large invertebrates such as cephalopods and crustaceans. With this approach, the movements and biology of thousands of marine creatures can be simultaneously monitored and studied in concert with oceanographic measurements. Results will significantly improve our understanding of the biology and behavior of migrating marine life, ocean physics modeling, and effects of climate change, and will advance resource management and international social and legal frameworks for ocean science.

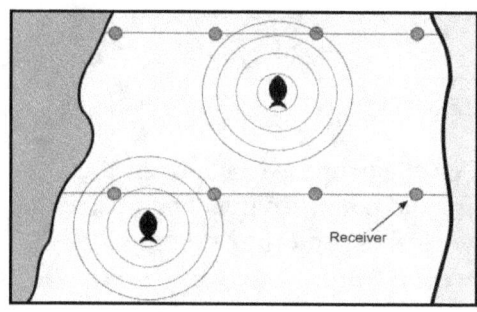

Fig. 1. Shore-to-slope "curtains" of acoustic receivers detect the passage of migratory fish. The fish can carry tags that archive information on past movements and oceanographic conditions, and the data can be downloaded to the receivers on acoustic contact. (Figure courtesy OTN)

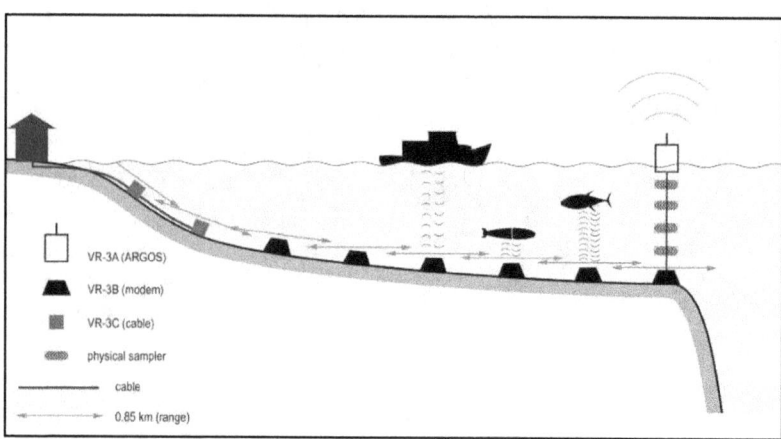

Fig. 2. Continuous "curtain" of receivers and samplers to simultaneously detect presence of tagged animals, download archived data from animals tags to array, and collect physical data. Data are retrieved by acoustic modem through the water column to a research vessel, by ARGOS satellite uplink, and/or by relay to shore station. (Figure courtesy OTN)

This worldwide initiative is spearheaded by Dalhousie University, which is securing the necessary equipment from Canadian manufacturers with approximately CAN$45M from the Canada Foundation of Innovation and Canada's National Science and Engineering Research Council (NSERC). Approximately 60 listening lines comprising 5,000 receivers are planned for 14 key ocean regions around the globe (Fig. 3). Included in these is a curtain crossing the Straits of Florida from Florida to Cuba, and an additional line crossing the Yucatan Channel from Mexico to Cuba (Fig. 4). Mote Marine Laboratory is the designated coordinating partner for deployment and operation of the Florida-Cuba OTN curtain and is also involved in helping to facilitate the Mexico-Cuba line.

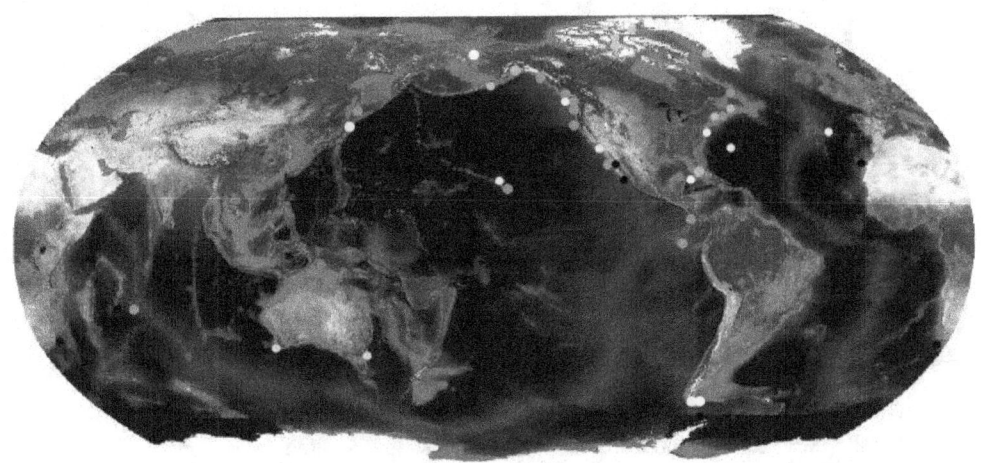

Fig. 3. Projected locations of OTN curtains in the world's oceans. Red dots = existing lines; orange = Phase 1 by 2009; yellow = Phase 2 by 2011; white = Phase 3 by 2012. (Figure courtesy OTN.)

For the Florida-Cuba curtain, a line of acoustic receivers and benthic pods will be deployed from the Florida Keys southward across the Straits of Florida. When complete, this sensory array will detect the presence of any acoustically tagged animal moving through the Straits of Florida, either out of or into the Gulf of Mexico. Data recorded include the presence of the individual animal, archived data from the animal's tag, and oceanographic measurements at the time of animal detection. Data accumulated by receivers will be uploaded to a shore-based station in one of three ways: 1) by acoustic modem through the water column on quarterly research cruises over the array; 2) by radio transmission to the ARGOS satellite system via surface transmitter; or 3) by "daisy-chaining" of receivers along the curtain to a landside receiving station in the Florida Keys. In this way, the array will not have to be pulled to the surface to retrieve archived data. Battery life of the receivers is approximately 4-7 years and the life expectancy of the overall array is projected to be 20 years. All data go to a centralized database where they are made freely available for all researchers involved. Proprietary nature of publishing rights for project-specific data is protected.

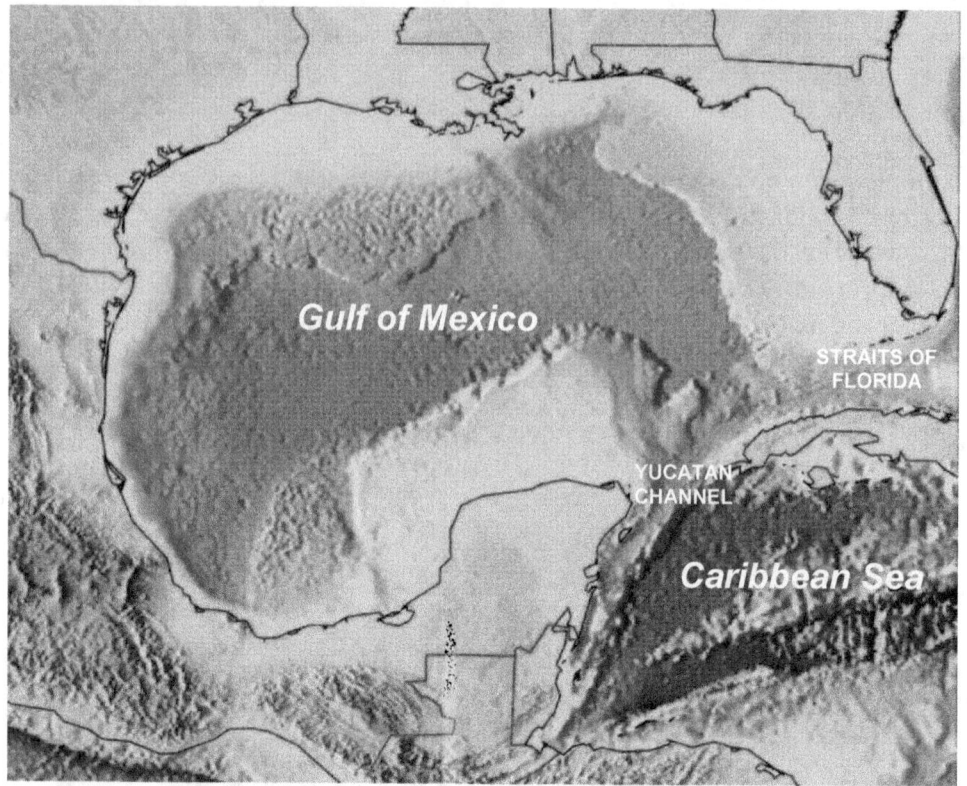

Fig. 4. The Gulf of Mexico and Caribbean Sea region showing the Straits of Florida, where the Florida-Cuba OTN line will be located, and the Yucatan Channel, where a Mexico-Cuba OTN line will be located. Primary current flow is northward through the Yucatan Channel from the Caribbean into the Gulf, and eastward through the Straits of Florida from the Gulf into the Atlantic Ocean.

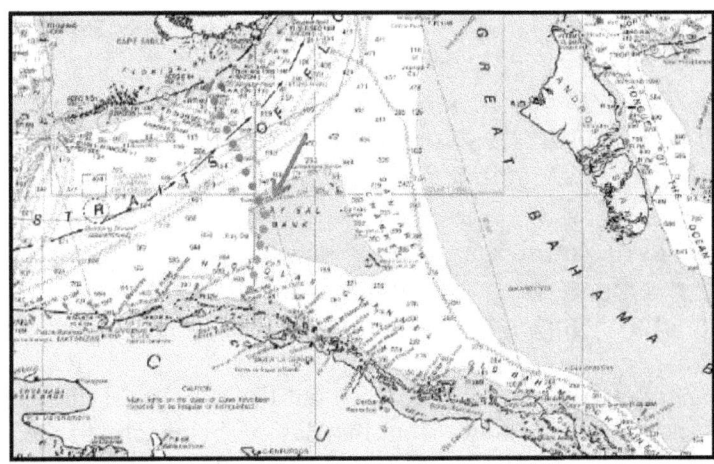

Fig. 5. OTN curtain off Florida Keys is projected to span the Straits of Florida, possibly running first to Cay Sal Bank in the Bahamas (arrow). Planning process currently underway will determine actual track.

The OTN approach provides a powerful tool for any scientist studying the movement of animals with acoustic transmitters, as well as for physical oceanographers interested in ocean dynamics. Once the Florida-Cuba and Mexico-Cuba lines are in place (projected to be by 2011), the two gateways to/from the Gulf of Mexico will be acoustically monitored at all times. This will provide a unique "front door, back door" array of biophysical sensors to detect upstream (through the Yucatan Channel) and downstream (through the Straits of Florida) conditions for the Islands in the Stream within the Gulf.

Challenges remaining for the deployment and operation of the Florida OTN include: 1) final identification of partners involved in the Florida curtain; 2) procurement of funds for deployment and operation (estimated to be $4M over five years of operations, to match $1.7M in equipment provided by OTN); and 3) political challenges of brokering the placement of sensors in Cuban territorial waters. These challenges are daunting but not insurmountable, and the enormous payoff of successful OTN operation at the Gulf's front and back doors will greatly benefit the state of ocean science in the region

Panel 6 Discussion

Libby Johns (NOAA Atlantic Oceanographic & Meteorological Lab) – presentation/panelist
John Wes Tunnell (The Harte Research Institute) – presentation/panelist
Bob Hueter (Mote Marine Laboratory) – presentation/panelist

(from meeting transcripts)

Al Hine: Any lingering effects from the big oil spill in the late 1970s?

Wes Tunnel: Yes you can see them but I'm not sure if there are any biological effects left. Took three months for it to get from the Bay of Campeche to the Texas gulf coast. Gave chance for studies before it got there. Can still see the oil line from the original spill. Tropical storm occurred and brought the oil over the reefs.

Liz Williams: OTN – Any analysis on how many species and seasonal coverage for the species you might be tagging?

Bob Hueter: Our role as coordinators is to get this tool in the water. This will be available to anyone doing acoustic tagging in the area. It's not necessarily our responsibility to coordinate the science. Dalhousie has worked out the details on the proprietary nature of the data. The sky is the limit. It's a completely open tool for everyone to use. We will want to coordinate regarding the physical dynamics as well. We're planning a workshop in the next couple of months. We have a little money from the state to get this going. Any one that has interest in this please let me know. I need to know what the interest is out there.

Julie Morris: What do we know about the connectivity about the currents in the Gulf?

Libby Johns: I don't know.

Wes Tunnel: I can give some anecdotal biological information. We have found 50 spiny lobsters on the jetty in Brownsville Texas – never there before, never there again. Some of this stuff is sporadic. It would be really neat to do the genetics on these things to find out where they are coming from.

Barbara Lausche: The Sian Ka'an Biosphere Reserve would pull in the reserve going down the chain? Are we going to get a multiplier effect here?

Wes Tunnell: Potentially. There are a few protected areas spread out. The no-take reserves are segments within the Sian Ka'an biosphere reserve. We need to be concerned about making it a broader network.

Tony Grogan: Were the Mexicans already doing this, or were they sparked to do more along with Islands in the Stream?

Wes Tunnell: They had already been doing this. The time is just right for making these work together.

Bob Hueter: The Mexican areas also include large tracts of land and have been in existence for a long time (20 years). They started as land protected areas with coastline and they are expanding the protection.

Jerry Ault: How far afield do those feeding/spawning aggregations go?

Bob Hueter: It's about 1000 sq km area total. It's a feeding area – no sign of spawning. They come there from May-September estimate ~1500 animals. Tagging shows they go all directions - into the gulf, into the Straits of Florida and into the Caribbean. The oceanography drives all of this. Libby's drifter data is very interesting – sometimes the sharks follow those same tracks, sometimes they go in their own direction.

Open Discussion

Moderator: Frank Alcock
Director, Mote Marine Policy Institute

(from meeting transcripts)

Five questions to toss out for the group to consider:

1. What do we know about the Gulf of Mexico as a Large Marine Ecosystem (in particular the sites identified)? What makes these sites ecologically unique?
2. Are we missing anything? Is there anything on that list that perhaps shouldn't be there?
3. What connects these sites? Do we know enough to say there is a robust inter-linkage with these areas?
4. What are the threats? Threats that aren't being adequately addressed in the existing governance structure?
5. What type of designation are we talking about here? What would that mean? What type of value added would we get from that designation? Some discussion possibly on process – although this admittedly was not the intention of this workshop.

Laura Geselbracht: I think this concept is a great one in terms of protecting biodiversity. We shouldn't limit ourselves to just fish and coral – we should expand the concept to include the full range of biodiversity – e.g. birds. The DeSoto Canyon is a unique feature – we have focused on things that stick up.

Ian MacDonald: I think we are missing deep water high productivity areas. The Gulf of Mexico is rich with deep-water resources. Same fauna in the deep area seep communities. There is connectivity demonstrated. There is connectivity in low energy environments.

Steve Atran: Hoping this concept will concentrate on – mentioned in earlier discussion – need long time series of data, limited data stations. We need to get out of this a data collection plan. We should ensure coordinated and ongoing data collection.

John Ogden: There is a sense of urgency that we shouldn't lose track of. These areas are essentially operating as refugia. Fishing, land based pollution and global climate change issues are making their way into these areas. If we think our own behavior is going to have an effect – "Islands in the Stream" is going to do that. It is happening out there, and it seems like it's going to get to these areas as well. Let's not monkey around with this.

Bob Weisberg: Having a set of these areas protected is a wonderful thought, but I think we should understand how these areas really work. If we are going to put together a science program – I want to see it aimed at that. We need to better understand these sites, a scientific program should be focused on them. All these efforts (e.g. the International Ocean Observing System [IOOS]) and none are making much progress. We are spinning our wheels. How do we simply not just put one more thing on the table? We need focus.
John Ogden: Want to respond to that from the MPA Advisory Committee and the Florida Keys.

This is a political activity and we need to put our resources into that. The science will get done if we have the focal areas. "Islands in the Stream" would provide this focus. These are previously vetted areas – these are our shot at getting something going and then building it. We're not going to get a science program to look at connectivity in the GOM. Place-based management can help focus science.

Billy Causey: We're talking about a MPA network – this is the broadest definition. We need to acknowledge the broadest definition of "marine protected area". We haven't decided whether this is no take. That will be done with other stakeholders involved too. Let's focus on what Bob said – we need the monitoring. That has to be ongoing. We have to know how we detect change. Take the physical and natural sciences and integrate them. We give you the rationale.

Jim Sinclair: What we are looking at here is the goal of trying to create a new entity to lead in this process. The idea is not to have an entity to sit inside all these others and do more different things. Instead to serve as a lead for these other groups that can be brought in as partners to support research and management. The idea should be to create a new entity to coordinate management and protection of the areas.

Barbara Lausche: I'm an Environmental Lawyer. I've worked on Protected Areas law all my life. My perspective – listening to scientists all day is half of what I do. I can't do my job unless I understand what is out there so I can understand what needs to be done. The US Legal system is the next step to take a breather and to be able to work thru your questions (the three John listed). We need to use the best legal instrument we have to protect these areas and to use that to let things slow down. As a political process – you throw in more than less, because you negotiate. Put it in and have it be part of your negotiating process and your filtering process until you get to the final product. Need a chance to use the best legal instrument (MPA) and use it. Also should be more inclusive.

Laura Geselbracht: We didn't hear a lot about socioeconomics today. But you are going to need that to understand what is at stake. What are the costs? What are the benefits? Need to understand these better.

Frank Alcock: I had a chance to speak with Billy & Dan about that, and agree that this aspect is important. A MPA will speak to regulating humans. We need a map that shows where human activity is occurring. Need as strong an effort on the social science side.

Tony Grogan: One of the premises is that this is a monument for George W. Bush. If he doesn't sign off on it, would it be carried over to the next administration?

Dan Basta: This is about you – it isn't about GW. It's up to you all to decide what needs to be done. If you leave it to the politicians, you are going to be unhappy. Interesting fact: many folks have said they've been doing what they've been doing for 35 years – meantime the US population has increased by 100 million people. So the world you started working in is very different from today. Can't develop strategies that are out of sync with time. US citizens are looking to the best and brightest, you, to tell them what to do. You have to decide how much info you need to step off the curb.

Ian MacDonald: Where are the nodes, where does the recruitment come from that would replenish these sites? Recruits from one spot could potentially replenish these areas – those potential seedbeds should be put at the top of the list.

Gene Shinn: (not entirely captured – related to the table created on size comparisons. Possibly a question about the size of the initiative.)

Wes Tunnell: The "Islands in the Stream" represents about 1/5 of 1% of the Gulf of Mexico. Would add .00196 sq miles of protected areas in the GOM. 1176 (Bill had 1136 sq mi) square miles. 35% smaller than all Texas bays and estuaries.

Wes Tunnell: We need to protect the ocean, what Billy & Dan are asking is: What are the areas that need to be protected? Years ago, Sylvia Earle went to some conference and reported that 12% of land is protected. Less than 1% of ocean is protected. We need to get more protection for the ocean.

Billy Causey: The point is, this is really small. We're not trying to have a large footprint – we're trying to protect the jewels around the gulf.

Villy Kourafalou: From the presentation and discussion we know enough to know that there is connection and that there is a need for action. It is clear that is a lot left to be learned. If you have a patient with a rare diseases, you don't wait, you do as much as you can and continue you research to see what more you can figure out. Enlarge the research to increase understanding. Although there is a lot to be learned and we need to do more research about the ecosystem and potential management activities, we still need to act now.

Paul Sammarco: We've talked about a lot of things today. One of the things I've learned in the last 7 years of working with gas platforms in the FGB area – spatial scale is important and effective conservation is important. Different organisms have different reproductive biology. More islands is better for starters. We can't declare too many islands, we can only define too few. We should be considering all potential sites at this early stage and (if necessary) narrow down the list following negotiation. Target organisms of concern must be taken into account in determining sites.

Jerry Ault: I'll preface my remarks by staying that I support any effort to enhance economic sustainability. However I'm stuck with the title of the document. Creating a network requires more meat in the process. Up front needs to be some level of risk analysis regarding the cost of *not* doing it. Need to conduct a risk analysis to determine value and benefits of the sites. Also understanding the efficacy of the process. Need to ensure follow-through to test results of protection. Needs some level of adaptivness. Hate to get into another conundrum that would undermine the science. Going to need science to support this proposal.

Dennis Heinemann: Commend Billy and the gang for what I think is a visionary proposal. We need to trust the science that we have and not worry so much about what we don't have. We know enough to get started. There are at least five reasons to do this: just protecting the areas themselves; we know at least from good theory that putting together a network will enhance ecological integrity at the gulf level; can help fisheries production; whether these small areas can do those or not, but the substance of the science is good enough. We are all committed to trying to do ecosystem-based management. And this is an opportunity to do that on a large scale. Finally this is the opportunity to do some international leadership on MPA networks. There is plenty of scientific reason to do this.

Mimi D'Iorio: Seawall issues in California – in hindsight we're taking these down – should have done some science before. There is a slew of georeferenced information – if we overlayed the data and allowed the computer to tell us the 15 best places – we would have the visual to make the case. If you overlay all these data, it makes it very clear to the non-scientists. This proposal is awesome, but if we could show what we know and what we are going to do next – it will look forward in filling the gaps that we already know are there. Proposal lacks demonstration of what we are going to do next.

Will Heyman: Functionality – I think what you are saying is absolutely so. This is ambitious, but it's not the first time people have gone about this. What people have learned is that management is not about the science, it's about changing behavior. We need to get the opposition on this on board ASAP. Having fishermen in Belize on board with protecting the aggregating fish – their voice is more powerful than the scientists.

Tony Grogan: I want to jump on that comment. I think this is what is missing here. I am from the fishing community. If it was done like Ducks Unlimited – where the hunters help make these decisions. Which of those areas is going to cause the biggest fight – I think it's going to be the Florida Middle Grounds. You're right – we have to get the fishermen on board. Need to include stakeholders in this process.

Dan Basta: How you have described that is exactly the way this needs to go. The process hasn't really started. The process is about people. That's what this is about. We're not going to influence the behavior of basking shark – it's to influence human behavior. But we haven't been given the green light to go ahead. If we get the green light to take this forward, we will have to slow them down so we can do the robust process. We can't let this go on the fast track. We have to be clear minded about how far we can take it – this is a continuous process. It becomes a social process of ownership. That ownership is key.

Bob Hueter: My interpretation is that the cart may be before the horse. Looking for scientific validation. We should provide scientific validation of this concept and no more. If we go this alone and this is a US initiative only – we've cut off the source. We really need to include those other places. Need to have a vision of an international effort from the very start. The scientific validity [of taking action] is weakened if Mexico and Belize are not included in the effort.

Julie Morris: Just based on today I don't think we've established the connectivity between the western Gulf and the rest of the area. I also want to plug for the hard bottom and live bottom on the West Florida Shelf. I think they are an important component of the stream that we're talking about.

Dennis Heinemann: Madison Swanson & Steamboat Lumps were established to look at the idea of protecting spawning males. That experiment hasn't worked as well as they wanted apparently due to poaching. A lot of people misunderstood the goals of those areas. It's important to recognize that this effort is about protecting the jewels – they can't exist in a vacuum. If we get any fishery benefit, that will be icing on the cake. These are too small. You'd need much larger areas to protect fisheries.

Lori Arguelles: Question regarding the Ducks Unlimited reference – what are the elements that can be translatable and can be used in this regard?

Tony Grogan: The strongest argument I heard today was what is going on in Mexico. Because that is downstream. I disagree with Julie about not enough connectivity – I learned about a lot of connectivity, and I was pretty skeptical. A lot of guys attack Billy & Chris Koenig – and I tell them these aren't bad people. I go out and work with Chris. We have to go out and work with the fishermen. We need to communicate better with fishermen about the international aspect of the project and the benefits to them (i.e., protecting sites "upstream")

Lori Arguelles: Are there any specific ways you would suggest that would help align fishermen and scientists?

Tony Grogan: The subject is complex about how to communicate and get people on board – and how to get other stakeholders to be communicating about a common goal of a sustainable environment.

Will Heyman: We work intimately with lots of commercial fishermen, and it seems to make a huge difference. You can watch a presentation, but a lot of people learn hands on. If you spend time in the field, there is a great exchange – fishermen have enhanced my science. Idea that it is really difficult to understand this type of thing unless they've seen this before – idea of exchange between fishermen from different sites to exchange of information. Detailed interviews of fishers.

Barbara Lausche: Heard today that there appears to be support for the concept in principle. There is support for the concept plus additional sites. It is important for us to come out with "something". If we are going to move in a process oriented way, need a schematic of best possible proposed selection as a base, from which there can be a discussion. How fast do NOAA and Dan need to have a recommendation from this meeting? Need to have the "best map" available before starting stakeholder process.

Andy Shepherd: This is big and important. We need to have faith in Sanctuary program. Don't forget Fisheries Management Council.

Steve Atran: You have to engage stakeholders and address their concerns. If not get support. 86,000 square miles of Gulf of Mexico already restricted but not coordinated. Draft discussion paper needs to be more explicit on goals and objectives, and how a coordinated system will reach these. Madison Swanson had enormous opposition. Once in place, once described clearly, a lot of opposition dropped away. Renewal supported almost by all.

Billy Causey: In 1992 I was hung in effigy, John's tires were slashed. Mistakes were made. We struggled in the mid 90's. We learned from that, and made adjustments to the final Management Plan based on public input. We came back in 1998 and started a new process to go forward and establish the Tortugas Ecological Reserve – we worked with 4 jurisdictions, any of which could have stopped the process. We started working with the commercial and recreational fishermen and went through the process. Four months before finalizing, Governor Bush said that if one commercial fishermen opposes, this won't happen. The program learned. The Office of National Marine Sanctuaries believe in people.

Frank Alcock: Has there been a lot more thought in the process, other than the brief 4 pager?

Dan Basta: Yes. Every time you do things like this, will be like it has never been done before. Creation process.

Dennis Heinemann: Try to learn what other people have done. Could learn what Great Barrier Reef Marine Park has done, and the California Marine Life Protection Act process. "How do you create array along coast that is ecologically connected?" asked. Can guarantee that this is connected, and also guarantee that it is not connected, based on the species. Interconnections based on the connections are going to ecological connect many species. Connection between sites may be stronger for some species than others.

Laura Geselbracht: Orders of magnitude and scale – differences between GBR and CA. Understand need to get "cream of crop", perhaps objectability of sustainability of ecosystems should be identified. Sustainability should be an objective

Emma Hickerson: We need a stand-alone document answering the questions of connectivity and representing a compilation about the state of existing knowledge.

Attendee List

This list of 84 attendees is incomplete and contains only speakers and invitees, and attendants who signed-in during the meeting:

Alcock	Frank	Mote Marine Laboratory	alcock@mote.org
Arguelles	Lori	National Marine Sanctuary Foundation	lori@nmsfocean.org
Armor	Jon	NOAA/NMS Headquarters	John.Armor@noaa.gov
Atran	Steven	Gulf of Mexico Fisheries Council	steven.atran@gulfcouncil.org
Ault	Jerry	University of Miami, RSMAS	jault@rsmas.miami.edu
Bailey	Michael	NOAA SE Regional Recreational Fisheries	Michael.Bailey@noaa.gov
Basta	Dan	NOAA/National Marine Sanctuary Program	Dan.Basta@noaa.gov
Beaver	Joel	Pritzker Marine Lab, New College of Florida	beaver@ncf.edu
Blaire	Jay	University of Miami, RSMAS	jblaire@rsmas.miami.edu
Borden	Larry	Manatee County Marine Advisory Board	radicalinc@aol.com
Brady	Margaret (Peg)	Council on Environmental Quality	mbrady@ceq.eop.gov
Brennan	Nate	Mote Marine Laboratory	nbrennan@mote.org
Burns	Karen	University of South Florida	k.burns@mote.org
Calderon	Rafael	The Nature Conservancy	rafael_calderon@tnc.org
Callahan	Mike	Fish and Wildlife Research Institute	michael.callahan@myfwc.com
Carollo	Cristina	Florida Institute of Oceanography	cristina.carollo@myfwc.com
Causey	Billy	NOAA/National Marine Sanctuary Program	billy.causey@noaa.gov
Cole	Brandon	Pritzker Marine Lab, New College of Florida	bcole@ncf.edu
Cozzi	COZ	Mote Marine Laboratory	coz@mote.org
Crabtree	Roy	NMFS, St. Petersburg	roy.crabtree@noaa.gov
Croom	Miles	NMFS Southeast Region	miles.croom@noaa.gov
Culliton	Tom	NOS/NOAA Special Projects	tom.culliton@noaa.gov
Culter	Jim	Mote Marine Laboratory	jculter@mote.org
Cunning	Ross	Mote Marine Laboratory	ross.cunning@gmail.com
D'Iorio	Mimi	NOAA/MPA Science Institute	mimi.diorio@noaa.gov
Estevez	Ernie	Mote Marine Laboratory	estevez@mote.org
Gannon	Janet	Mote Marine Laboratory	jangann@mote.org
Geselbracht	Laura	The Nature Conservancy	lgeselbracht@tnc.org
Grimes	Shepherd	NOAA General Council	shepherd.grimes@noaa.gov
Grogan	Tony	Spearboard.com	enter@bellsouth.net
Heil	Cindy	Fish and Wildlife Research Institute	cindy.heil@myfwc.com
Heinemann	Dennis	Ocean Conservancy	Dheinemann@oceanconservancy.org
Hendee	Jim	NOAA/AOML	Jim.Hendee@noaa.gov
Hueter	Bob	Mote Marine Laboratory	rhueter@mote.org
Heyman	Will	Texas A&M University	wheyman@tamu.edu
Hickerson	Emma	FGBNMS	Emma.Hickerson@noaa.gov
Hine	Al	USF Marine Sciences	hine@marine.usf.edu
Hogarth	Bill	USF Marine Sciences	Bill.Hogarth@noaa.gov
Houser	Letise	National Marine Sanctuary Foundation	letise@nmsfocean.org
Jaap	Walt	University of South Florida CMS	wjaap@tampabay.rr.com
Johns	Libby	NOAA/AOML	libby.johns@noaa.gov
Keller	Brian	NOAA/National Marine Sanctuary Program	brian.keller@noaa.gov
Kiene	Bill	NOAA/National Marine Sanctuary Program	William.Kiene@noaa.gov
Koenig	Chris	Institute for Fishery Resource Ecology, FSU	koenig@bio.fsu.edu
Kourafalou	Villy	University of Miami RSMAS	Vkourafalou@rsmas.miami.edu

Kuffner	Ilsa	USGS, St. Petersburg FL	ikuffner@usgs.gov
Lausche	Barbara	Mote Marine Laboratory	blausche@mote.org
Lorenzen	Kai	Imperial College London	k.lorenzen@imperial.ac.uk
Mahadevan	Kumar	Mote Marine Laboratory	kumar@mote.org
McDonald	Ian	Harte Research Institute, TAMUCC	ian.macdonal@tamucc.edu
Morris	Julie	New College of Florida	morris@ncf.edu
Morton	Sean	NOAA/NMS Headquarters	sean.morton@noaa.gov
Ogden	John	Florida Institute of Oceanography	jogden@seas.marine.usf.edu
O'Mara	Dana	Mote Marine Laboratory	danaomara@mote.org
Palandro	David	Fish and Wildlife Research Institute	david.palandro@myfwc.com
Pierce	Richard	Mote Marine Laboratory	rich@mote.org
Ponwith	Bonnie	NOAA Southeast Fisheries Science Center	bonnie.ponwith@noaa.gov
Precht	Bill	Battelle Memorial Institute	PrechtW@battelle.org
Reed	Dave	Florida Institute of Oceanography	DaveReed@myfwc.com
Reich	Christopher	USGS, St. Petersburg FL	creich@usgs.gov
Ritchie	Kim	Mote Marine Laboratory	ritchie@mote.org
Rogers	Alice	Imperial College London	a.rogers07@imperial.ac.uk
Sammarco	Paul	Louisiana Universities Marine Consortium	psammarco@lumcon.edu
Score	Dave	NOAA/FKNMS	David.A.Score@noaa.gov
Shen	Glen	Mote Marine laboratory	glenshen@mote.org
Shepard	Andrew	NURC/UNCW	sheparda@uncw.edu
Shinn	Gene	University of South Florida CMS	eshinn@marine.usf.edu
Sinclair	Jim	Mineral Management Services	James.Sinclair@mms.gov
Slowey	Niall	Texas A&M University	slowey@ocean.tamu.edu
Stevely	John	Sea Grant Marine Extension	jmstevely@ifas.ufl.edu
Struve	Juliane	Mote Marine Laboratory	juliane_struve@yahoo.co.uk
Sutter	Buck	NMFS, St. Petersburg	Buck.Sutter@noaa.gov
Tanner	Brad	Mote Marine Laboratory	brad.tanner@mote.org
Thurmond	Joel	Mote Marine Laboratory	thurmond@mote.org
Tunnell	Wes	Harte Research Institute, TAMUCC	wes.tunnell@tamucc.edu
Vaughan	Dave	Mote Marine Laboratory	dvaughan@mote.org
Weaver	Doug	Flower Garden Banks NMS	doug.weaver@noaa.gov
Wedel	Jim	Manatee Sea Grant Advisory Committee	vitsea@earthlink.net
Weisberg	Bob	University of South Florida CMS	weisberg@marine.usf.edu
Wells	Martha	Mote Marine Laboratory	mwells@mote.org
Wetzel	Dana	Mote Marine Laboratory	dana@mote.org
White	David	Ocean Conservancy	dwhite@oceanconservancy.org
Williams	Liz	AOML/RSMAS	ewilliams@rsmas.miami.edu
Wilmot	Fiona	Keys Connectivity Inc.	fionawilmont@earthlink.net

Appendix A: HAPC and Other Habitat or Area Based Regulations
(January 17, 2008)

Shepherd Grimes
NOAA General Council, NMFS, St. Petersburg FL

§ 600.810 Definitions and word usage.
(a) . . .

Habitat areas of particular concern means those areas of EFH identified pursuant to §600.815(a)(8).

§ 600.815 Contents of Fishery Management Plans.

 (a) Mandatory contents- . . .

 (8) Identification of habitat areas of particular concern. FMPs should identify specific types or areas of habitat within EFH as habitat areas of particular concern based on one or more of the following considerations:

(i) The importance of the ecological function provided by the habitat.

(ii) The extent to which the habitat is sensitive to human-induced environmental degradation.

(iii) Whether, and to what extent, development activities are, or will be, stressing the habitat type.

(iv) The rarity of the habitat type.

§ 622.2 Definitions and acronyms.

Gulf and South Atlantic prohibited coral means, in the Gulf and South Atlantic, one or more of the following, or a part thereof:

(1) Coral belonging to the Class Hydrozoa (fire corals and hydrocorals).

(2) Coral belonging to the Class Anthozoa, Subclass Hexacorallia, Orders Scleractinia (stony corals) and Antipatharia (black corals).

(3) A seafan, *Gorgonia flabellum* or *G. ventalina.*

(4) Coral in a coral reef, except for allowable octocoral.

(5) Coral in an HAPC, including allowable octocoral.

HAPC means habitat area of particular concern.

§ 622.34   Gulf EEZ seasonal and/or area closures.

(a) Alabama SMZ. The Alabama SMZ consists of artificial reefs and surrounding areas. In the Alabama SMZ, fishing by a vessel that is operating as a charter vessel or headboat, a vessel that does not have a commercial permit for Gulf reef fish, as required under §622.4(a)(2), or a vessel with such a permit fishing for Gulf reef fish is limited to hook-and-line gear with three or fewer hooks per line and spearfishing gear. A person aboard a vessel that uses on any trip gear other than hook-and-line gear with three or fewer hooks per line and spearfishing gear in the Alabama SMZ is limited on that trip to the bag limits for Gulf reef fish specified in §622.39(b) and, for Gulf reef fish for which no bag limit is specified in §622.39(b), the vessel is limited to 5 percent, by weight, of all fish on board or landed. The Alabama SMZ is bounded by rhumb lines connecting, in order, the following points:

Point	North lat.	West long.
A	30°02.5'	88°07.7'
B	30°02.6'	87°59.3'
C	29°55.0'	87°55.5'
D	29°54.5'	88°07.5'
A	30°02.5'	88°07.7'

(b) Florida middle grounds HAPC. Fishing with a bottom longline, bottom trawl, dredge, pot, or trap is prohibited year round in the area bounded by rhumb lines connecting, in order, the following points:

Point	North lat.	West long.
A	28°42.5'	84°24.8'
B	28°42.5'	84°16.3'
C	28°11.0'	84°00.0'
D	28°11.0'	84°07.0'
E	28°26.6'	84°24.8'
A	28°42.5'	84°24.8'

(c) Reef fish longline and buoy gear restricted area. A person aboard a vessel that uses, on any trip, longline or buoy gear in the longline and buoy gear restricted area is limited on that trip to the bag limits for Gulf reef fish specified in §622.39(b)(1) and, for Gulf reef fish for which no bag limit is specified in §622.39(b)(1), the vessel is limited to 5 percent, by weight, of all fish on board or landed. The longline and buoy gear restricted area is that part of the Gulf EEZ shoreward of rhumb lines connecting, in order, the points listed in Table 1, in Appendix B of this part.

(d) Tortugas marine reserves HAPC. The following activities are prohibited within the Tortugas marine reserves HAPC: Fishing for any species and bottom anchoring by fishing vessels.

(1) EEZ portion of Tortugas North. The area is bounded by rhumb lines connecting the following points: From point A at 24°40'00" N. lat., 83°06'00" W. long. to point B at 24°46'00" N. lat.,

83°06'00" W. long. to point C at 24°46'00" N. lat., 83°00'00" W. long.; thence along the line denoting the seaward limit of Florida's waters, as shown on the current edition of NOAA chart 11434, to point A at 24°40'00" N. lat., 83°06'00" W. long.

(2) Tortugas South. The area is bounded by rhumb lines connecting, in order, the following points:

Point	North lat.	West long.
A	24°33'00"	83°09'00"
B	24°33'00"	83°05'00"
C	24°18'00"	83°05'00"
D	24°18'00"	83°09'00"
A	24°33'00"	83°09'00"

(e) Shrimp/stone crab separation zones. Five zones are established in the Gulf EEZ and Florida's waters off Citrus and Hernando Counties for the separation of shrimp trawling and stone crab trapping. Although Zone II is entirely within Florida's waters, it is included in this paragraph (e) for the convenience of fishermen. Restrictions that apply to Zone II and those parts of the other zones that are in Florida's waters are contained in Rule 46–38.001, Florida Administrative Code. Geographical coordinates of the points referred to in this paragraph (e) are as follows:

Point	North lat.	West long.
A	28°59'30"	82°45'36"
B	28°59'30"	83°00'10"
C	28°26'01"	82°59'47"
D	28°26'01"	82°56'54"
E	28°41'39"	82°55'25"
F	28°41'39"	82°56'09"
G	28°48'56"	82°56'19"
H	28°53'51"	82°51'19"
I1	28°54'43"	82°44'52"
J2	28°51'09"	82°44'00"
K	28°50'59"	82°54'16"
L	28°41'39"	82°53'56"
M3	28°41'39"	82°38'46"
N	28°41'39"	82°53'12"
O	28°30'51"	82°55'11"
P	28°40'00"	82°53'08"
Q	28°40'00"	82°47'58"
R	28°35'14"	82°47'47"
S	28°30'51"	82°52'55"
T	28°27'46"	82°55'09"
U	28°30'51"	82°52'09"

1Crystal River Entrance Light 1A.
2Long Pt. (southwest tip).
3Shoreline.

(1) Zone I is enclosed by rhumb lines connecting, in order, points A, B, C, D, T, E, F, G, H, I, and J, plus the shoreline between points A and J. It is unlawful to trawl in that part of Zone I that is in the EEZ from October 5 through May 20, each year.

(2) Zone II is enclosed by rhumb lines connecting, in order, points J, I, H, K, L, and M, plus the shoreline between points J and M.

(3) Zone III is enclosed by rhumb lines connecting, in order, points P, Q, R, U, S, and P. It is unlawful to trawl in that part of Zone III that is in the EEZ from October 5 through May 20, each year.

(4) Zone IV is enclosed by rhumb lines connecting, in order, points E, N, S, O, and E.

(i) It is unlawful to place a stone crab trap in that part of Zone IV that is in the EEZ from October 5 through December 1 and from April 2 through May 20, each year.

(ii) It is unlawful to trawl in that part of Zone IV that is in the EEZ from December 2 through April 1, each year.

(5) Zone V is enclosed by rhumb lines connecting, in order, points F, G, K, L, and F.

(i) It is unlawful to place a stone crab trap in that part of Zone V that is in the EEZ from October 5 through November 30 and from March 16 through May 20, each year.

(ii) It is unlawful to trawl in that part of Zone V that is in the EEZ from December 1 through March 15, each year.

(f) Southwest Florida seasonal trawl closure. From January 1 to 1 hour after official sunset on May 20, each year, trawling, including trawling for live bait, is prohibited in that part of the Gulf EEZ shoreward of rhumb lines connecting, in order, the following points:

Point	North lat.	West long.
B1	26°16.0'	81°58.5'
C	26°00.0'	82°04.0'
D	25°09.0'	81°47.6'
E	24°54.5'	81°50.5'
M1	24°49.3'	81°46.4'

1On the seaward limit of Florida's waters.

(g) Reef fish stressed area. The stressed area is that part of the Gulf EEZ shoreward of rhumb lines connecting, in order, the points listed in Table 2, in Appendix B of this part.

(1) A powerhead may not be used in the stressed area to take Gulf reef fish. Possession of a powerhead and a mutilated Gulf reef fish in the stressed area or after having fished in the stressed area constitutes prima facie evidence that such reef fish was taken with a powerhead in

the stressed area. The provisions of this paragraph do not apply to the following species: dwarf sand perch, hogfish, and sand perch.

(2) A roller trawl may not be used in the stressed area. Roller trawl means a trawl net equipped with a series of large, solid rollers separated by several smaller spacer rollers on a separate cable or line (sweep) connected to the footrope, which makes it possible to fish the gear over rough bottom, that is, in areas unsuitable for fishing conventional shrimp trawls. Rigid framed trawls adapted for shrimping over uneven bottom, in wide use along the west coast of Florida, and shrimp trawls with hollow plastic rollers for fishing on soft bottoms, are not considered roller trawls.

(3) A fish trap may not be used in the stressed area. A fish trap used in the stressed area will be considered unclaimed or abandoned property and may be disposed of in any appropriate manner by the Assistant Administrator (including an authorized officer).

(h) Texas closure. (1) From 30 minutes after official sunset on May 15 to 30 minutes after official sunset on July 15, trawling, except trawling for royal red shrimp beyond the 100-fathom (183-m) depth contour, is prohibited in the Gulf EEZ off Texas.

(2) In accordance with the procedures and restrictions of the Fishery Management Plan for the Shrimp Fishery of the Gulf of Mexico, the RA may adjust the closing and/or opening date of the Texas closure to provide an earlier, later, shorter, or longer closure, but the duration of the closure may not exceed 90 days or be less than 45 days. Notification of the adjustment of the closing or opening date will be published in theFederal Register.

(i) Tortugas shrimp sanctuary. (1) The Tortugas shrimp sanctuary is closed to trawling. The Tortugas shrimp sanctuary is that part of the EEZ off Florida shoreward of rhumb lines connecting, in order, the following points:

Point	North lat.	West long.
N1	25°52.9'	81°37.9'
F	24°50.7'	81°51.3'
G2	24°40.1'	82°26.7'
H3	24°34.7'	82°35.2'
P4	24°35.0'	82°08.0'

1Coon Key Light.
2New Ground Rocks Light.
3Rebecca Shoal Light.
4Marquessas Keys.

(2) The provisions of paragraph (i)(1) of this section notwithstanding—

(i) Effective from April 11 through September 30, each year, that part of the Tortugas shrimp sanctuary seaward of rhumb lines connecting the following points is open to trawling: From point T at 24°47.8' N. lat., 82°01.0' W. long. to point U at 24°43.83' N. lat., 82°01.0' W. long. (on the line denoting the seaward limit of Florida's waters); thence along the seaward limit of

Florida's waters, as shown on the current edition of NOAA chart 11439, to point V at 24°42.55' N. lat., 82°15.0' W. long.; thence north to point W at 24°43.6' N. lat., 82°15.0' W. long.

(ii) Effective from April 11 through July 31, each year, that part of the Tortugas shrimp sanctuary seaward of rhumb lines connecting the following points is open to trawling: From point W to point V, both points as specified in paragraph (i)(2)(i) of this section, to point G, as specified in paragraph (i)(1) of this section.

(iii) Effective from May 26 through July 31, each year, that part of the Tortugas shrimp sanctuary seaward of rhumb lines connecting the following points is open to trawling: From point F, as specified in paragraph (i)(1) of this section, to point Q at 24°46.7' N. lat., 81°52.2' W. long. (on the line denoting the seaward limit of Florida's waters); thence along the seaward limit of Florida's waters, as shown on the current edition of NOAA chart 11439, to point U and north to point T, both points as specified in paragraph (i)(2)(i) of this section.

(j) West and East Flower Garden Banks HAPC. The following activities are prohibited year-round in the HAPC: Fishing with a bottom longline, bottom trawl, buoy gear, dredge, pot, or trap and bottom anchoring by fishing vessels.

(1) West Flower Garden Bank. West Flower Garden Bank is bounded by rhumb lines connecting, in order, the following points:

Point	North lat.	West long.
A	27°55'22.8"	93°53'09.6"
B	27°55'22.8"	93°46'46.0"
C	27°49'03.0"	93°46'46.0"
D	27°49'03.0"	93°53'09.6"
A	27°55'22.8"	93°53'09.6"

(2) East Flower Garden Bank. East Flower Garden Bank is bounded by rhumb lines connecting, in order, the following points:

Point	North lat.	West long.
A	27°59'14.4"	93°38'58.2"
B	27°59'14.4"	93°34'03.5"
C	27°52'36.5"	93°34'03.5"
D	27°52'36.5"	93°38'58.2"
A	27°59'14.4"	93°38'58.2"

(k) Closure provisions applicable to the Madison and Swanson sites and Steamboat Lumps. (1)(i) The Madison and Swanson sites are bounded by rhumb lines connecting, in order, the following points:

Point	North lat.	West long.
A	29°17'	85°50'
B	29°17'	85°38'
C	29°06'	85°38'
D	29°06'	85°50'
A	29°17'	85°50'

(ii) Steamboat Lumps is bounded by rhumb lines connecting, in order, the following points:

Point	North lat.	West long.
A	28°14'	84°48'
B	28°14'	84°37'
C	28°03'	84°37'
D	28°03'	84°48'
A	28°14'	84°48'

(iii) The provisions of paragraphs (k)(2) through (6) of this section apply within the Madison and Swanson sites and Steamboat Lumps through June 16, 2010.

(2) Possession of Gulf reef fish is prohibited, except for such possession aboard a vessel in transit with fishing gear stowed as specified in paragraph (k)(4) of this section.

(3) During November through April, all fishing is prohibited, and possession of any fish species is prohibited, except for such possession aboard a vessel in transit with fishing gear stowed as specified in paragraph (k)(4) of this section. The provisions of this paragraph, (k)(3), do not apply to highly migratory species.

(4) For the purpose of paragraph (k) of this section, transit means non-stop progression through the area; fishing gear appropriately stowed means -

(i) A longline may be left on the drum if all gangions and hooks are disconnected and stowed below deck. Hooks cannot be baited. All buoys must be disconnected from the gear; however, buoys may remain on deck.

(ii) A trawl net may remain on deck, but trawl doors must be disconnected from the trawl gear and must be secured.

(iii) A gillnet must be left on the drum. Any additional gillnets not attached to the drum must be stowed below deck.

(iv) A rod and reel must be removed from the rod holder and stowed securely on or below deck. Terminal gear (i.e., hook, leader, sinker, flasher, or bait) must be disconnected and stowed separately from the rod and reel. Sinkers must be disconnected from the down rigger and stowed separately.

(5) During May through October, surface trolling is the only allowable fishing activity. For the purpose of this paragraph (k)(5), surface trolling is defined as fishing with lines trailing behind a vessel which is in constant motion at speeds in excess of four knots with a visible wake. Such trolling may not involve the use of down riggers, wire lines, planers, or similar devices.

(6) For the purpose of paragraph (k) of this section, fish means finfish, mollusks, crustaceans, and all other forms of marine animal and plant life other than marine mammals and birds. Highly

migratory species means tuna species, marlin (*Tetrapturus* spp. and *Makaira* spp .), oceanic sharks, sailfishes (*Istiophorus* spp .), and swordfish (*Xiphias gladius*).

(l) [Reserved]

(m) Closures of the recreational fishery for red snapper. The recreational fishery for red snapper in or from the Gulf EEZ is closed from January 1 through April 20 and from November 1 through December 31. During a closure, the bag and possession limit for red snapper in or from the Gulf EEZ is zero.

(n) Seasonal closure of the commercial fishery for vermilion snapper. The commercial fishery for vermilion snapper in or from the Gulf EEZ is closed from April 22 through May 31, each year. During the closure, no person aboard a vessel for which a valid Federal commercial permit for Gulf reef fish has been issued may fish for or possess vermilion snapper in the Gulf, regardless of where harvested. However, a person aboard a vessel for which the permit indicates both charter vessel/headboat for Gulf reef fish and commercial Gulf reef fish may continue to retain vermilion snapper under the bag and possession limits specified in §622.39(b)(1)(v) and (b)(2), respectively, provided the vessel is operating as a charter vessel or headboat. During the closure, the sale or purchase of vermilion snapper is prohibited as specified in §622.45(c)(5).

(o) Seasonal closure of the commercial fishery for gag, red grouper, and black grouper. From February 15 to March 15, each year, no person aboard a vessel for which a valid Federal commercial permit for Gulf reef fish has been issued may possess gag, red grouper, or black grouper in the Gulf, regardless of where harvested. From February 15 until March 15, each year, the sale or purchase of gag, red grouper, or black grouper is prohibited as specified in §622.45(c)(4).

(p) Closures of the Gulf group king mackerel gillnet fishery. The gillnet fishery for Gulf group king mackerel in or from the Gulf EEZ is closed each fishing year from July 1 until 6:00 a.m. on the day after the Martin Luther King Jr. Federal holiday. The gillnet fishery also is closed during all subsequent weekends and observed Federal holidays, except for the first weekend following the Martin Luther King Jr. holiday which will remain open to the gillnet fishery provided a notification of closure of that fishery has not been filed under §622.43(a). Weekend closures are effective from 6:00 a.m. Saturday to 6:00 a.m. Monday. Holiday closures are effective from 6:00 a.m. on the observed Federal holiday to 6:00 a.m. the following day. All times are eastern standard time. During these closures, a person aboard a vessel using or possessing a gillnet with a stretched-mesh size of 4.75 inches (12.1 cm) or larger in the southern Florida west coast subzone may not fish for or possess Gulf group king mackerel.

(q) [Reserved]

(r) Pulley Ridge HAPC. Fishing with a bottom longline, bottom trawl, buoy gear, pot, or trap and bottom anchoring by fishing vessels are prohibited year-round in the area of the HAPC bounded by rhumb lines connecting, in order, the following points:

Point	North lat.	West long.
A	24°58'18"	83°38'33"

B	24°58'18"	83°37'00"
C	24°41'11"	83°37'00"
D	24°40'00"	83°41'22"
E	24°43'55"	83°47'15"
A	24°58'18"	83°38'33"

(s) Stetson Bank HAPC. Fishing with a bottom longline, bottom trawl, buoy gear, pot, or trap and bottom anchoring by fishing vessels are prohibited year-round in the HAPC, which is bounded by rhumb lines connecting, in order, the following points:

Point	North lat.	West long.
A	28°10'38.3"	94°18'36.5"
B	28°10'38.3"	94°17'06.3"
C	28°09'18.6"	94°17'06.3"
D	28°09'18.6"	94°18'36.5"
A	28°10'38.3"	94°18'36.5"

(t) McGrail Bank HAPC. Fishing with a bottom longline, bottom trawl, buoy gear, pot, or trap and bottom anchoring by fishing vessels are prohibited year-round in the HAPC, which is bounded by rhumb lines connecting, in order, the following points:

Point	North lat.	West long.
A	27°59'06.0"	92°37'19.2"
B	27°59'06.0"	92°32'17.4"
C	27°55'55.5"	92°32'17.4"
D	27°55'55.5"	92°37'19.2"
A	27°59'06.0"	92°37'19.2"

(u) Seasonal closure of the recreational fishery for gag, red grouper, and black grouper. The recreational fishery for gag, red grouper, and black grouper in or from the Gulf EEZ is closed from February 15 to March 15, each year. During the closure, the bag and possession limit for gag, red grouper, and black grouper in or from the Gulf EEZ is zero.

Currently proposed regulatory changes

622.34 Gulf EEZ seasonal and/or area closures.

(l) Closures of the Gulf shrimp fishery to reduce red snapper bycatch. During a closure implemented in accordance with this paragraph (l), trawling is prohibited within the specified closed area(s).

(1) Procedure for determining need for and extent of closures. Each year, in accordance with the applicable framework procedure established in the FMP for the Shrimp Fishery in the Gulf of Mexico (FMP), the RA will, if necessary, establish a seasonal area closure for the shrimp fishery in all or a portion of the areas of the Gulf EEZ specified in paragraphs (l)(2) through (l)(4) of this section. The RA's determination of the need for such closure and its geographical scope and duration will be based on an annual assessment, by the Southeast Fisheries Science Center, of the shrimp effort and associated shrimp trawl bycatch mortality on red snapper in the 1030 fathom area of statistical zones 1021, compared to the 74-percent target reduction of shrimp trawl bycatch mortality on red snapper from the benchmark years of 20012003 established in the FMP. The framework procedure provides for adjustment of this target reduction level, consistent with the red snapper stock rebuilding plan and the findings of subsequent stock assessments, via appropriate rulemaking. The assessment will be based on shrimp effort data for the most recent 12-month period available and will include a recommendation regarding the geographical scope and duration of the closure. The Southeast Fisheries Science Centers assessment will be provided to the RA on or about March 1 of each year. If the RA determines that a closure is necessary, the closure falls within the scope of the potential closures evaluated in the FMP, and good cause exists to waive notice and comment, NMFS will implement the closure by publication of a final rule in the Federal Register. If such good cause waiver is not justified, NMFS will implement the closure via appropriate notice and comment rulemaking. NMFS intends that any closure implemented consistent with this paragraph (l) will begin on the same date and time as the Texas closure.

(2) Eastern zone. The eastern zone is bounded by rhumb lines connecting, in order, the following points:

Point	North lat.	West long.
A	29° 14'	88° 57'
B	29° 24'	88° 34'
C	29° 34'	87° 38'
D	30° 04'	87° 00'
E	30° 04'	88° 41'
F	29° 36'	88° 37'
G	29° 21'	88° 59'
A	29° 14'	88° 57'

(3) *Louisiana zone.* The Louisiana zone is bounded by rhumb lines connecting, in order, the following points:

Point	North lat.	West long.
A	29° 09.1'	93° 41.4'
B	29° 09.25'	92° 36'
C	28° 35'	90° 44'
D	29° 09'	89° 48'
E	28° 57'	89° 34'
F	28° 40'	90° 09'
G	28° 18'	90° 33'
H	28° 25'	91° 37'
I .	28° 21.7'	93° 28.4'
A	29° 09.1'	93° 41.4'

(4) *Texas zone.* The Texas zone is bounded by rhumb lines connecting, in order, the following points:

Point	North lat.	West long.
A	29° 09.1'	93° 41.4'
B	28° 44'	95° 15'
C	28° 11'	96° 17'
D	27° 44'	96° 53'
E	27° 02'	97° 11'
F	26° 00.5'	96° 57.3'
G	26° 00.5'	96° 35.85'
H	26° 24'	96° 36'
I .	26° 49'	96° 52'
J .	27° 12'	96° 51'
K	27° 39'	96° 33'
L	27° 55'	96° 04'
M	28° 21.7'	93° 28.4'
A	29° 09.1'	93° 41.4'

(m) The recreational fishery for red snapper in or from the Gulf EEZ is closed from January 1 through May 31 and from October 1 through December 31, each year.

NMSP CONSERVATION SERIES PUBLICATIONS

To date, the following reports have been published in the Marine Sanctuaries Conservation Series. All publications are available on the National Marine Sanctuary Program website (http://www.sanctuaries.noaa.gov/).

M/V *ELPIS* Coral Reef Restoration Monitoring Report Monitoring Events 2004-2007 Florida Keys National Marine Sanctuary Monroe County, Florida (NMSP-08-03)

CONNECTIVITY Science, People and Policy in the Florida Keys National Marine Sanctuary (NMSP-08-02)

M/V *ALEC OWEN MAITLAND* Coral Reef Restoration Monitoring Report Monitoring Events 2004-2007 Florida Keys National Marine Sanctuary Monroe County, Florida (NMSP-08-01)

Automated, objective texture segmentation of multibeam echosounder data - Seafloor survey and substrate maps from James Island to Ozette Lake, Washington Outer Coast. (NMSP-07-05)

Observations of Deep Coral and Sponge Assemblages in Olympic Coast National Marine Sanctuary, Washington (NMSP-07-04)

A Bioregional Classification of the Continental Shelf of Northeastern North America for Conservation Analysis and Planning Based on Representation (NMSP-07-03)

M/V *WELLWOOD* Coral Reef Restoration Monitoring Report Monitoring Events 2004-2006 Florida Keys National Marine Sanctuary Monroe County, Florida (NMSP-07-02)

Survey report of NOAA Ship McArthur II cruises AR-04-04, AR-05-05 and AR-06-03: Habitat classification of side scan sonar imagery in support of deep-sea coral/sponge explorations at the Olympic Coast National Marine Sanctuary (NMSP-07-01)

2002 - 03 Florida Keys National Marine Sanctuary Science Report: An Ecosystem Report Card After Five Years of Marine Zoning (NMSP-06-12)

Habitat Mapping Effort at the Olympic Coast National Marine Sanctuary - Current Status and Future Needs (NMSP-06-11)

M/V *CONNECTED* Coral Reef Restoration Monitoring Report Monitoring Events 2004-2005 Florida Keys National Marine Sanctuary Monroe County, Florida (NMSP-06-010)

M/V *JACQUELYN L* Coral Reef Restoration Monitoring Report Monitoring Events 2004-2005 Florida Keys National Marine Sanctuary Monroe County, Florida (NMSP-06-09)

M/V *WAVE WALKER* Coral Reef Restoration Baseline Monitoring Report - 2004 Florida Keys National Marine Sanctuary Monroe County, Florida (NMSP-06-08)

Olympic Coast National Marine Sanctuary Habitat Mapping: Survey report and classification of side scan sonar data from surveys HMPR-114-2004-02 and HMPR-116-2005-01 (NMSP-06-07)

A Pilot Study of Hogfish (*Lachnolaimus maximus* Walbaum 1792) Movement in the Conch Reef Research Only Area (Northern Florida Keys) (NMSP-06-06)

Comments on Hydrographic and Topographic LIDAR Acquisition and Merging with Multibeam Sounding Data Acquired in the Olympic Coast National Marine Sanctuary (ONMS-06-05)

Conservation Science in NOAA's National Marine Sanctuaries: Description and Recent Accomplishments (ONMS-06-04)

Normalization and characterization of multibeam backscatter: Koitlah Point to Point of the Arches, Olympic Coast National Marine Sanctuary - Survey HMPR-115-2004-03 (ONMS-06-03)

Developing Alternatives for Optimal Representation of Seafloor Habitats and Associated Communities in Stellwagen Bank National Marine Sanctuary (ONMS-06-02)

Benthic Habitat Mapping in the Olympic Coast National Marine Sanctuary (ONMS-06-01)

Channel Islands Deep Water Monitoring Plan Development Workshop Report (ONMS-05-05)

Movement of yellowtail snapper (Ocyurus chrysurus Block 1790) and black grouper (Mycteroperca bonaci Poey 1860) in the northern Florida Keys National Marine Sanctuary as determined by acoustic telemetry (MSD-05-4)

The Impacts of Coastal Protection Structures in California's Monterey Bay National Marine Sanctuary (MSD-05-3)

An annotated bibliography of diet studies of fish of the southeast United States and Gray's Reef National Marine Sanctuary (MSD-05-2)

Noise Levels and Sources in the Stellwagen Bank National Marine Sanctuary and the St. Lawrence River Estuary (MSD-05-1)

Biogeographic Analysis of the Tortugas Ecological Reserve (MSD-04-1)

A Review of the Ecological Effectiveness of Subtidal Marine Reserves in Central California (MSD-04-2, MSD-04-3)

Pre-Construction Coral Survey of the M/V Wellwood Grounding Site (MSD-03-1)

Olympic Coast National Marine Sanctuary: Proceedings of the 1998 Research Workshop, Seattle, Washington (MSD-01-04)

Workshop on Marine Mammal Research & Monitoring in the National Marine Sanctuaries (MSD-01-03)

A Review of Marine Zones in the Monterey Bay National Marine Sanctuary (MSD-01-2)

Distribution and Sighting Frequency of Reef Fishes in the Florida Keys National Marine Sanctuary (MSD-01-1)

Flower Garden Banks National Marine Sanctuary: A Rapid Assessment of Coral, Fish, and Algae Using the AGRRA Protocol (MSD-00-3)

The Economic Contribution of Whalewatching to Regional Economies: Perspectives From Two National Marine Sanctuaries (MSD-00-2)

Olympic Coast National Marine Sanctuary Area to be Avoided Education and Monitoring Program (MSD-00-1)

Multi-species and Multi-interest Management: an Ecosystem Approach to Market Squid (*Loligo opalescens*) Harvest in California (MSD-99-1)